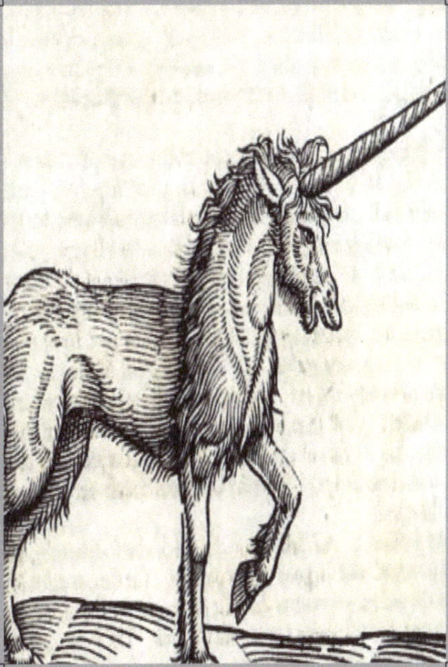

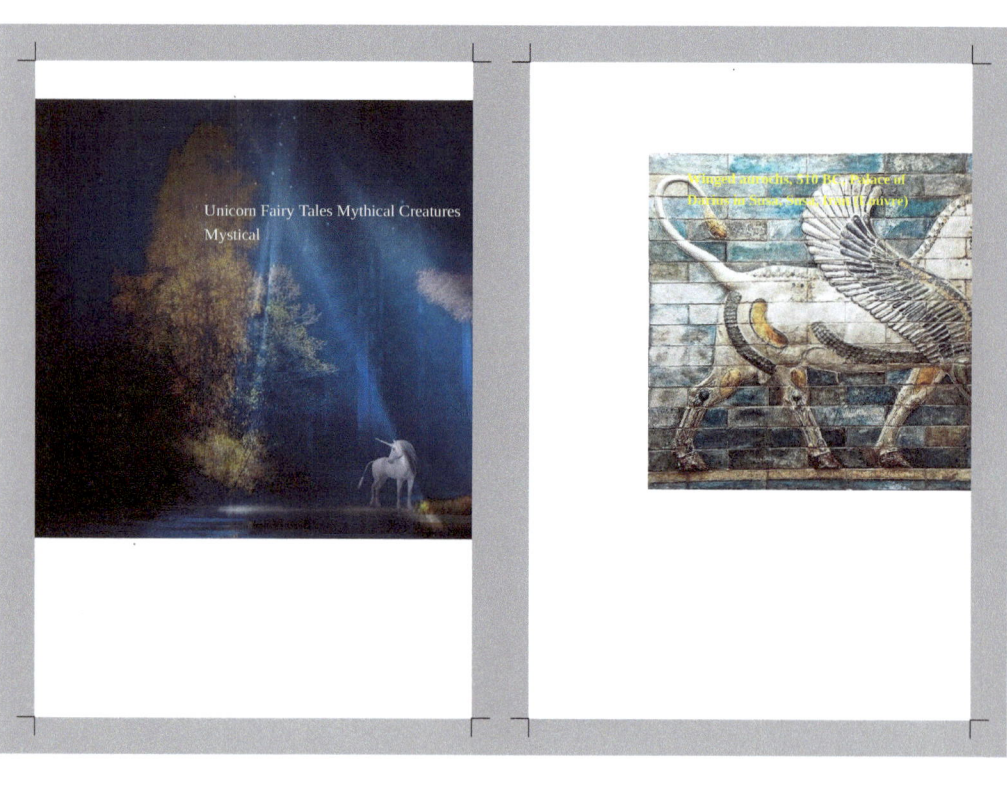

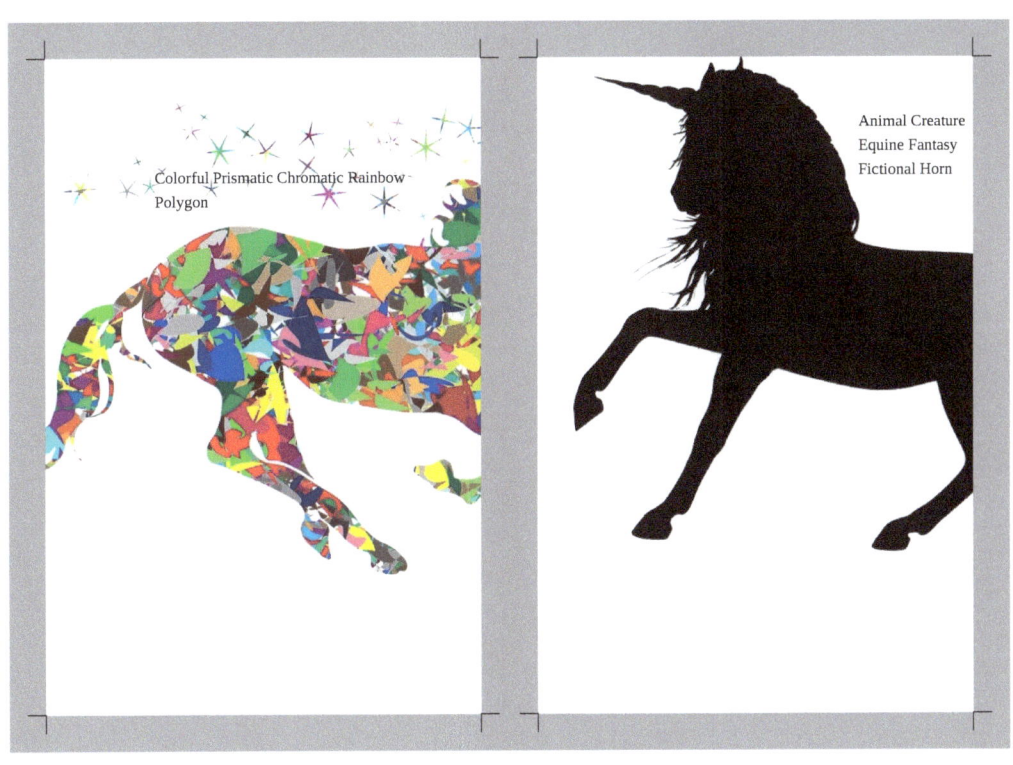

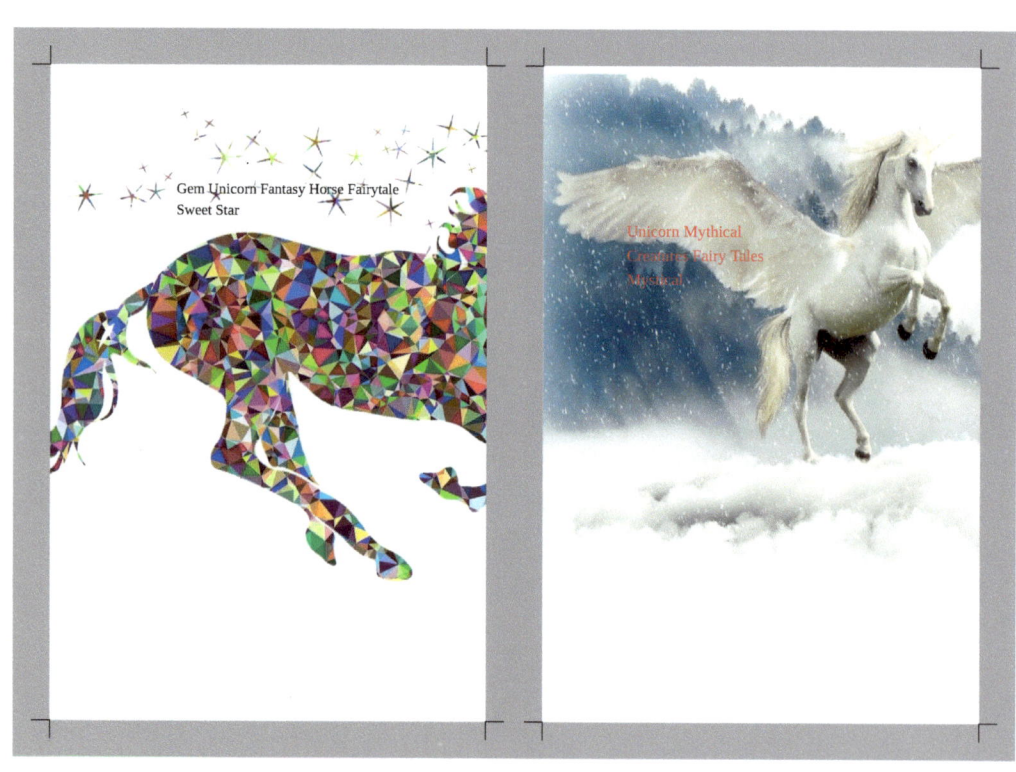

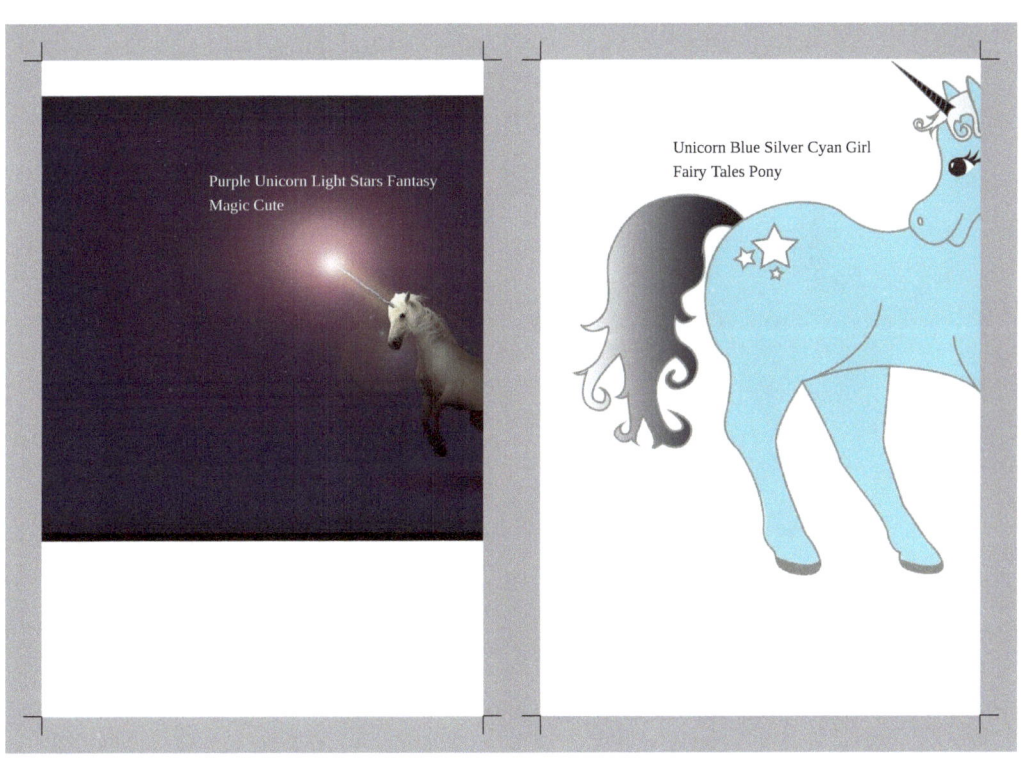

Unicorn Mythical Creatures Mane White Horn Toon

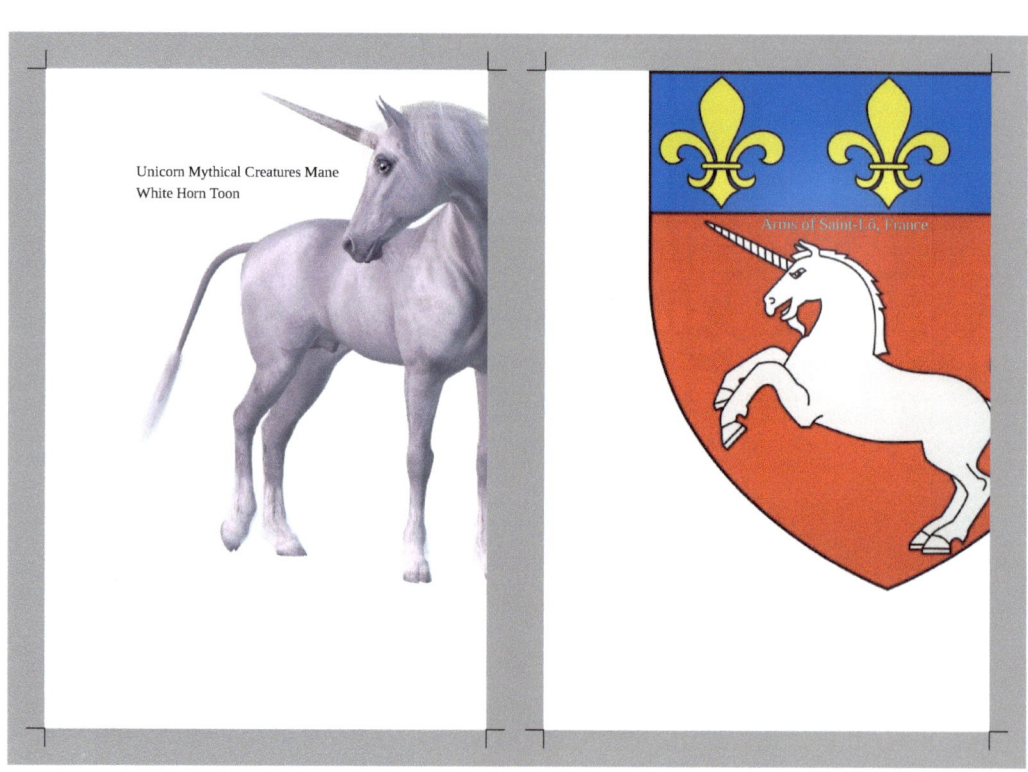

Arms of Saint-Lô, France

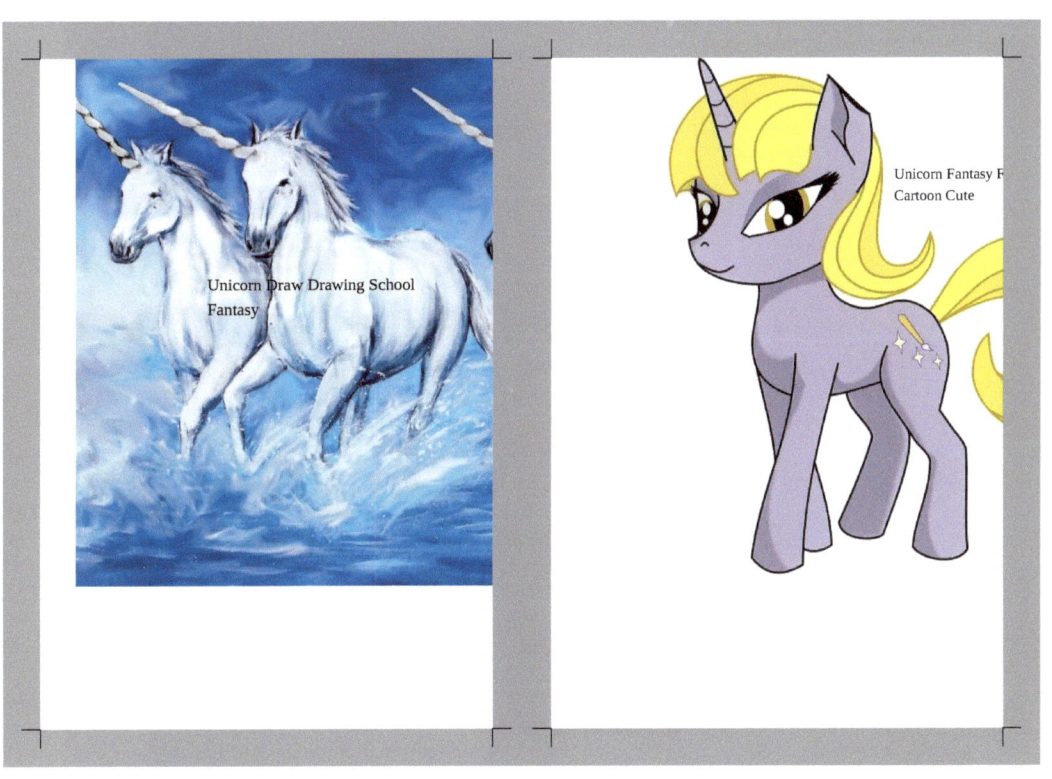

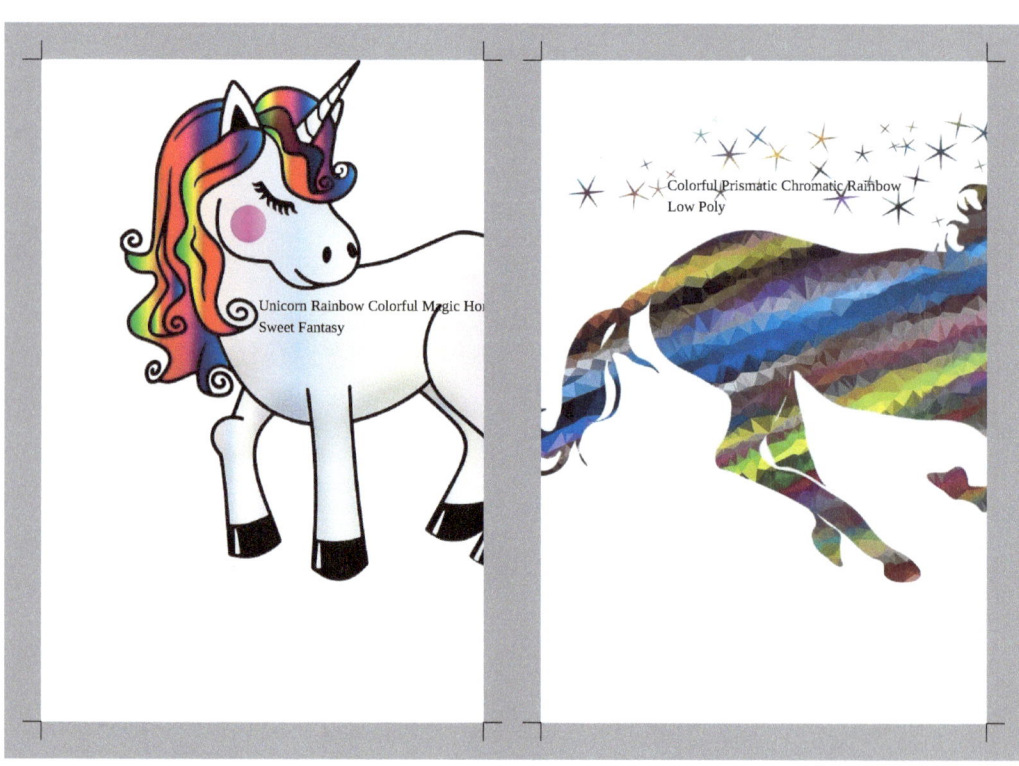

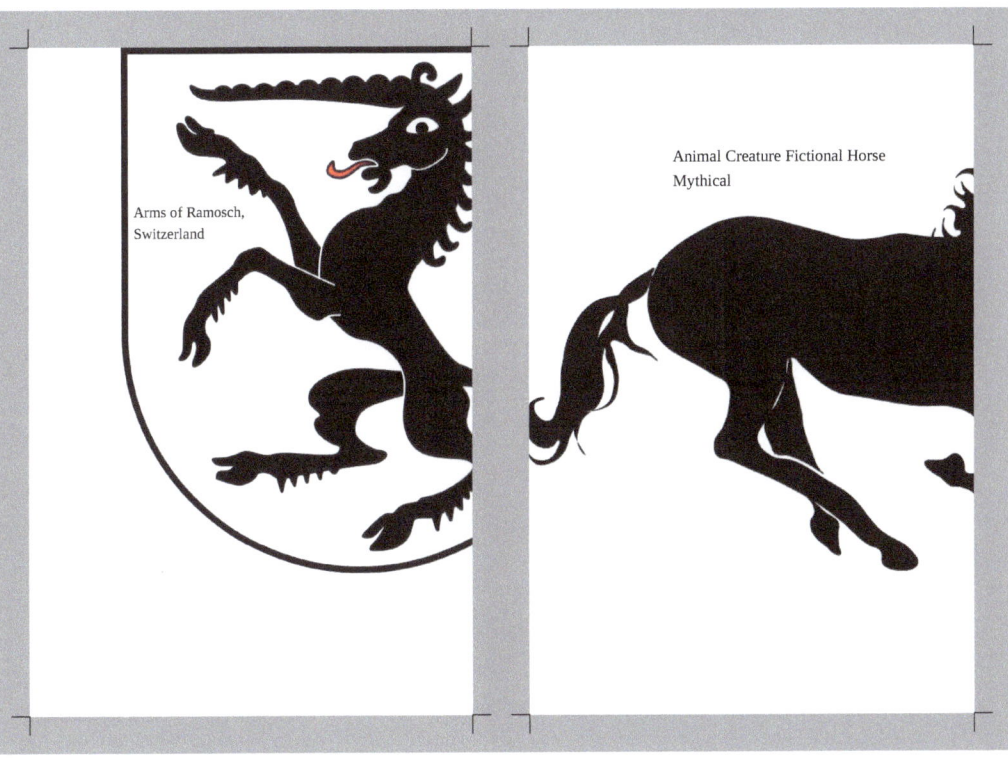

Arms of Ramosch, Switzerland

Animal Creature Fictional Horse Mythical

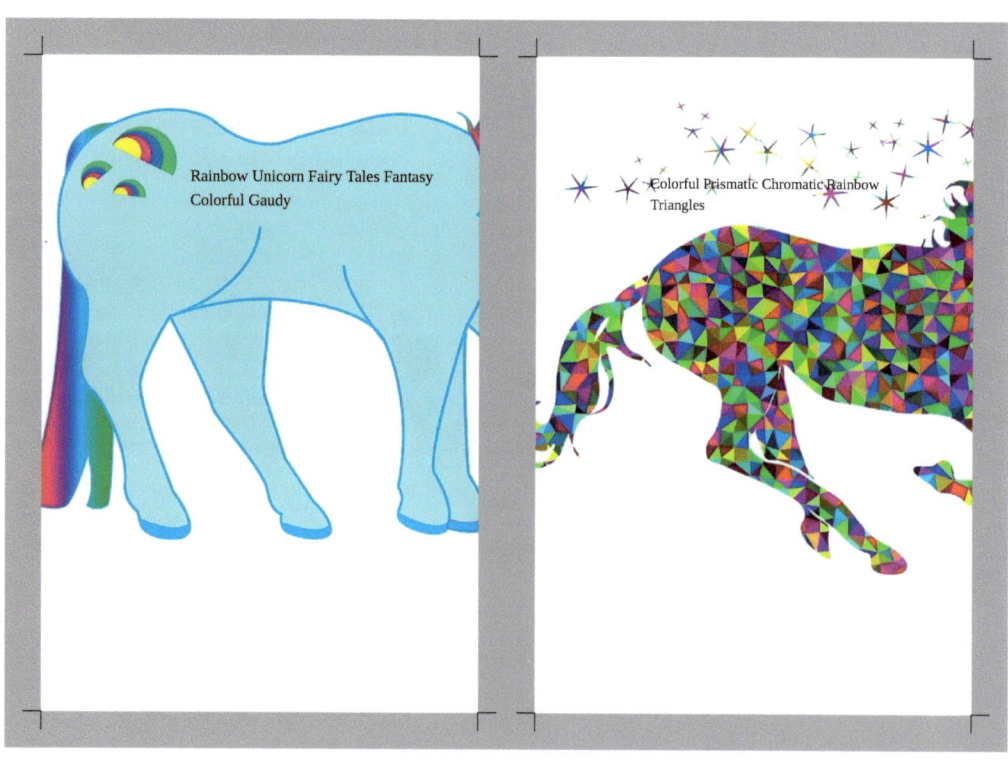

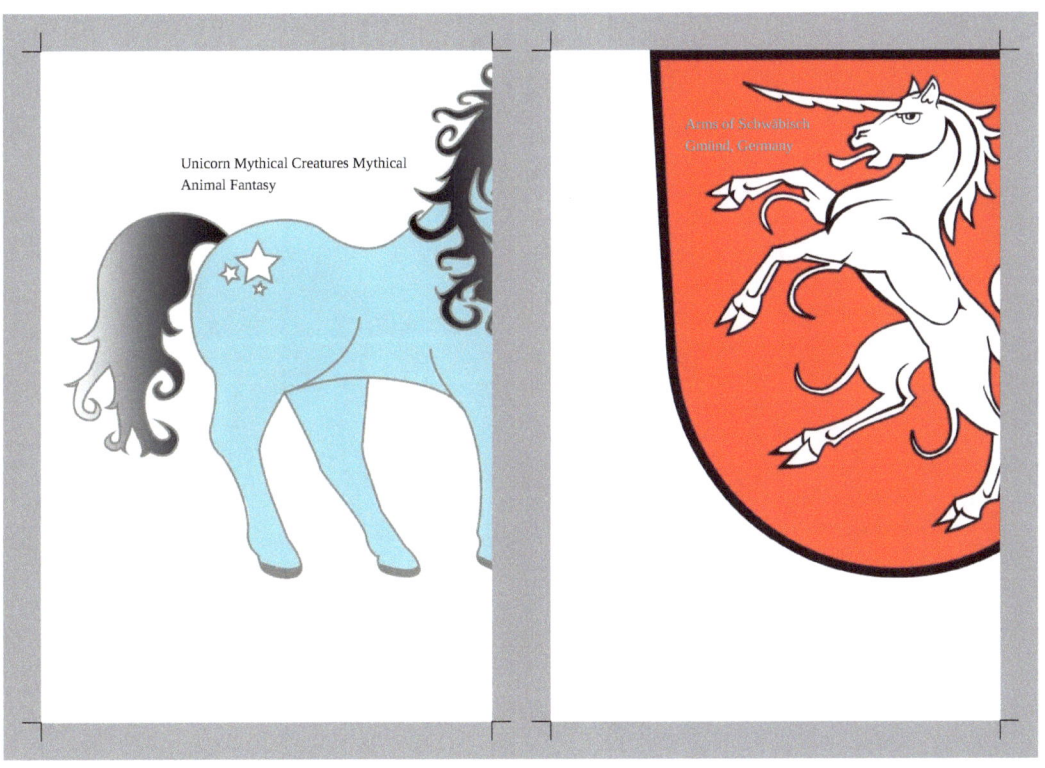

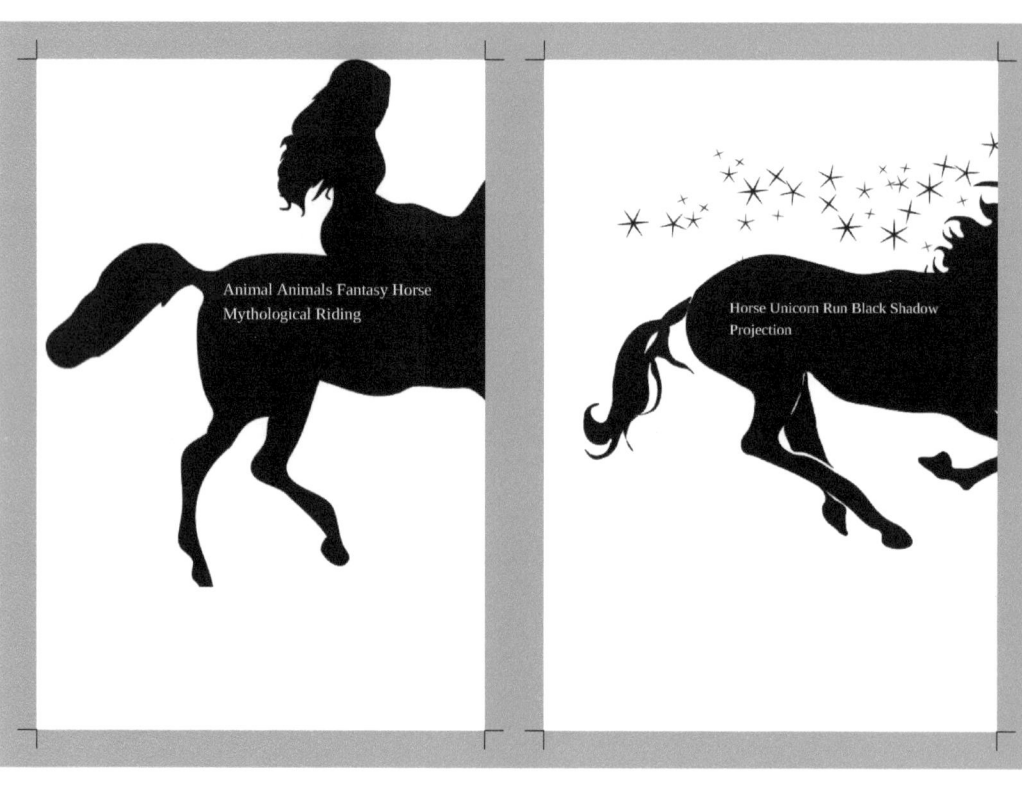

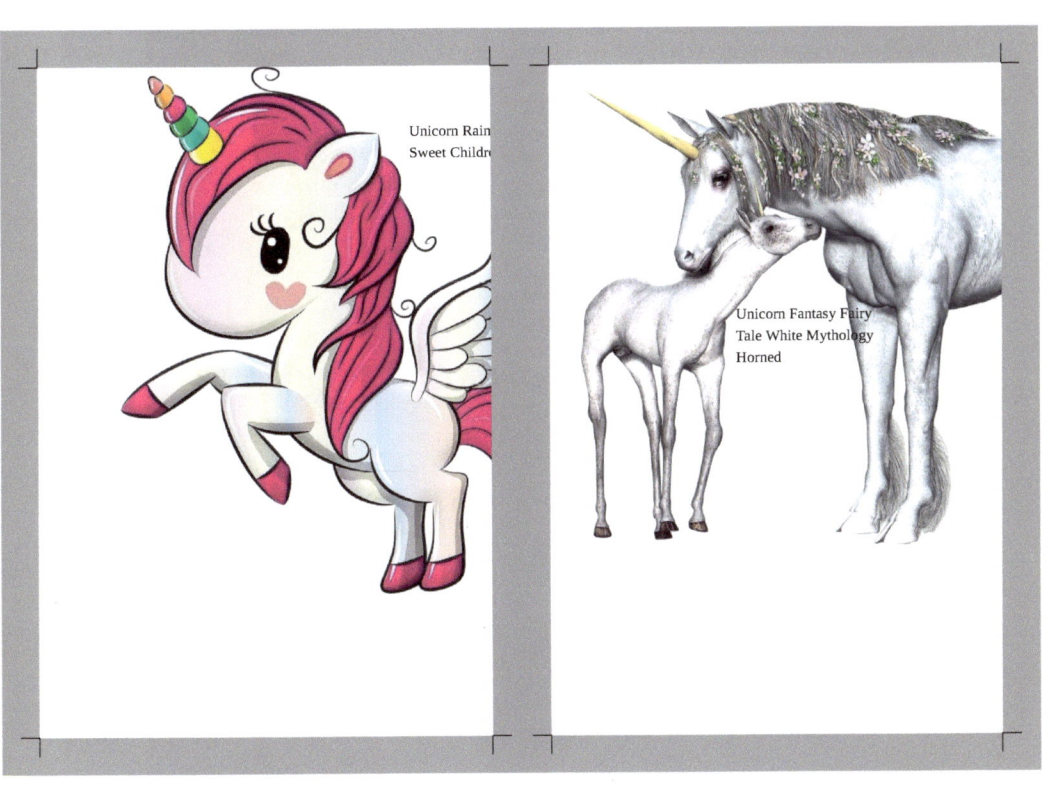

Unicorn Rainbow Sweet Children

Unicorn Fantasy Fairy Tale White Mythology Horned

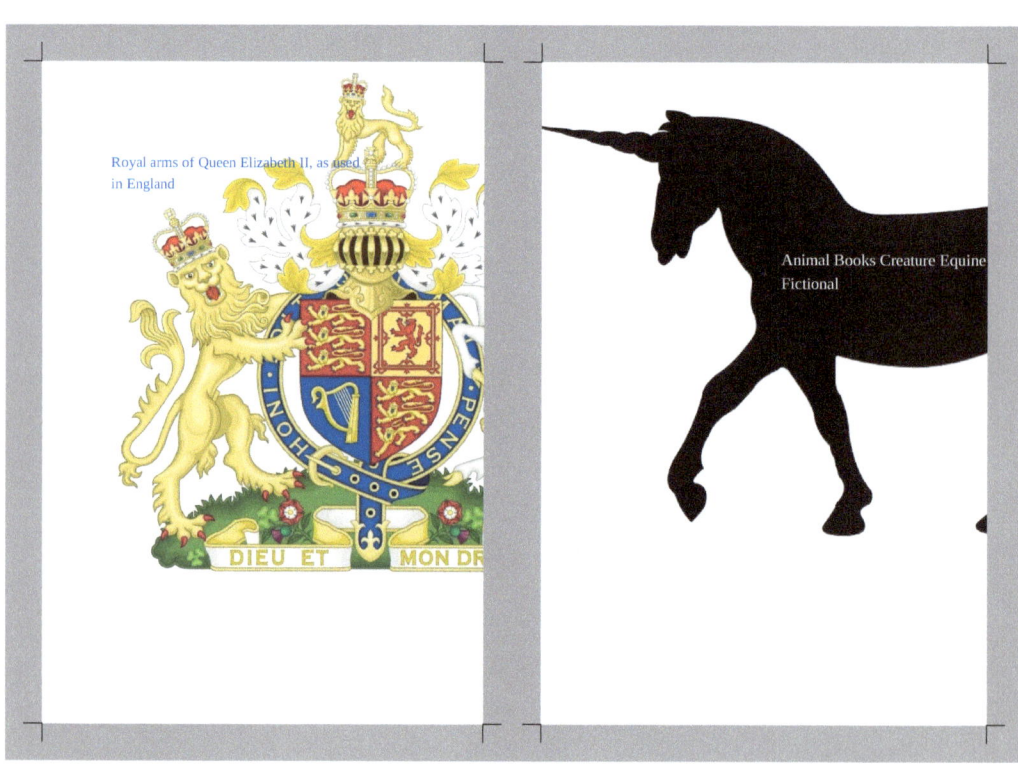

Royal arms of Queen Elizabeth II, as used in England

Animal Books Creature Equine Fictional

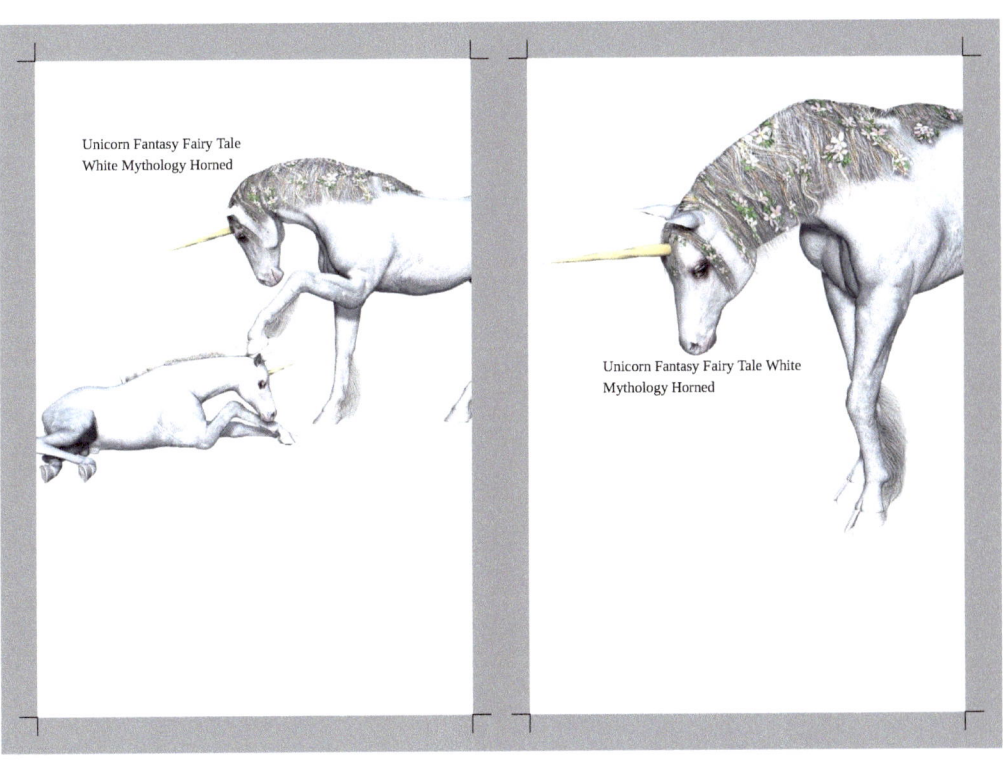

Animal Fictional Head
Horse Mythical Silhouette

Animal Horse Equine Mammal Pets
Equestrian Tube

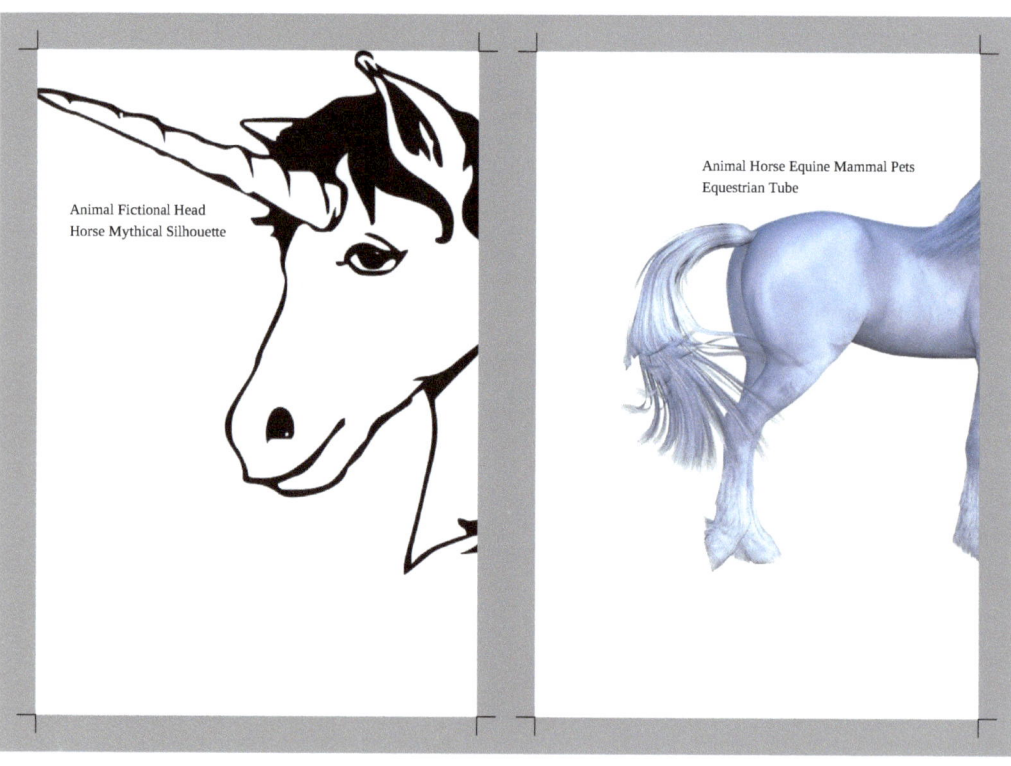

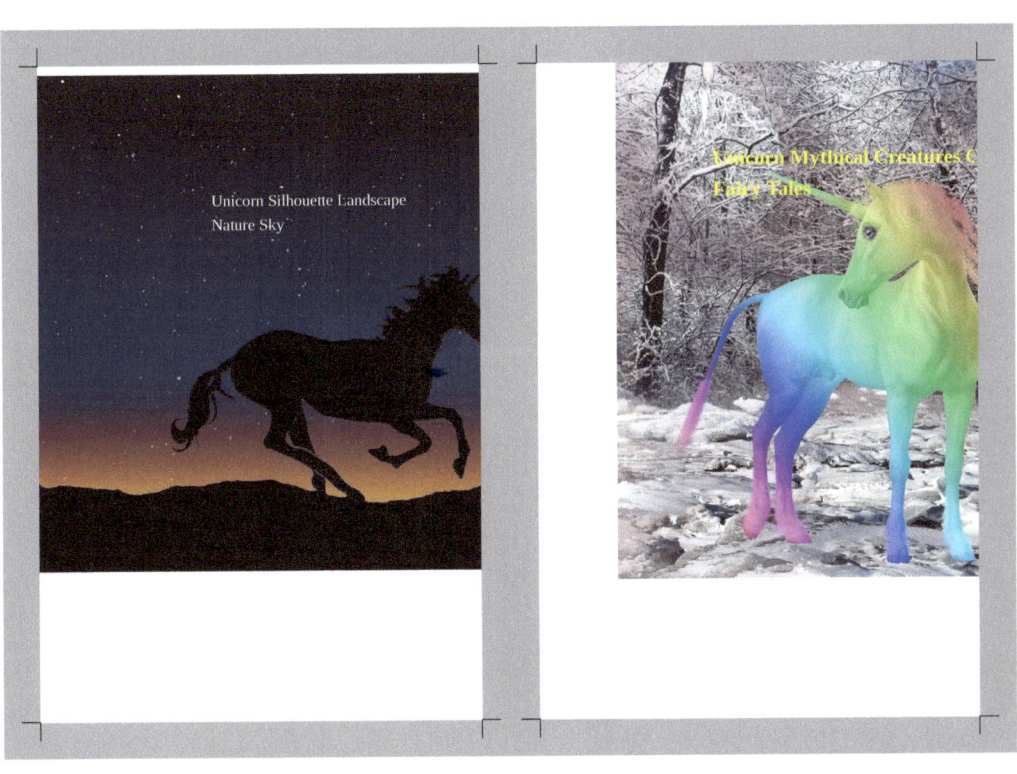

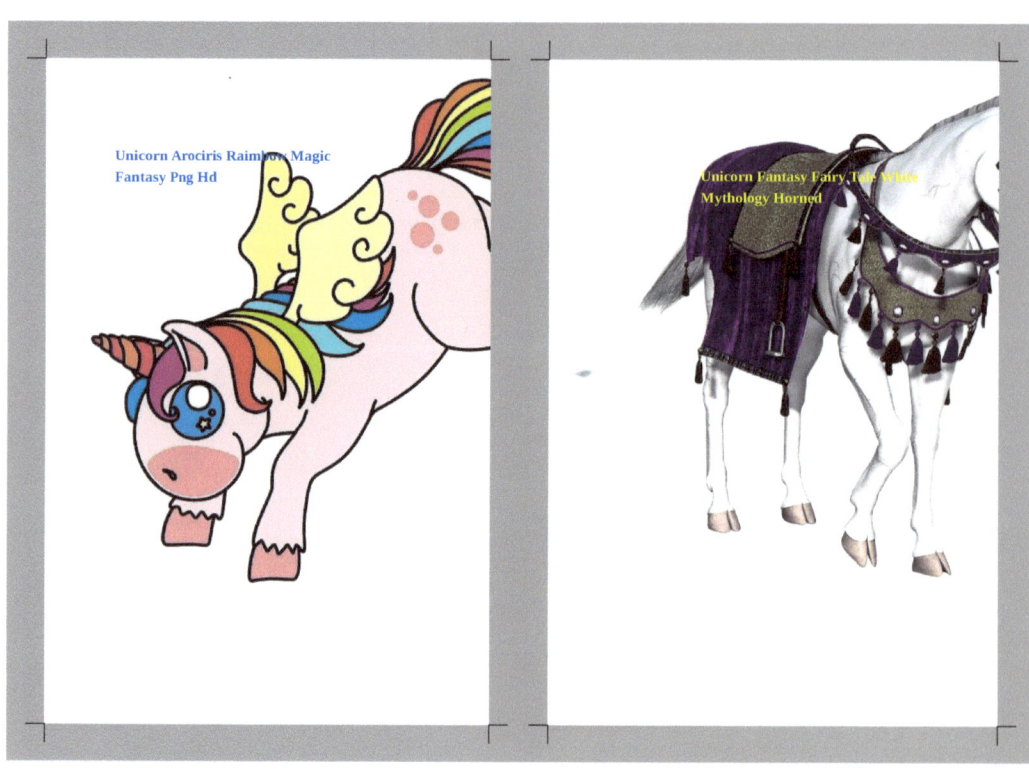

Unicorn Arociris Raimbow Magic Fantasy Png Hd

Unicorn Fantasy Fairy Tale Wilde Mythology Horned

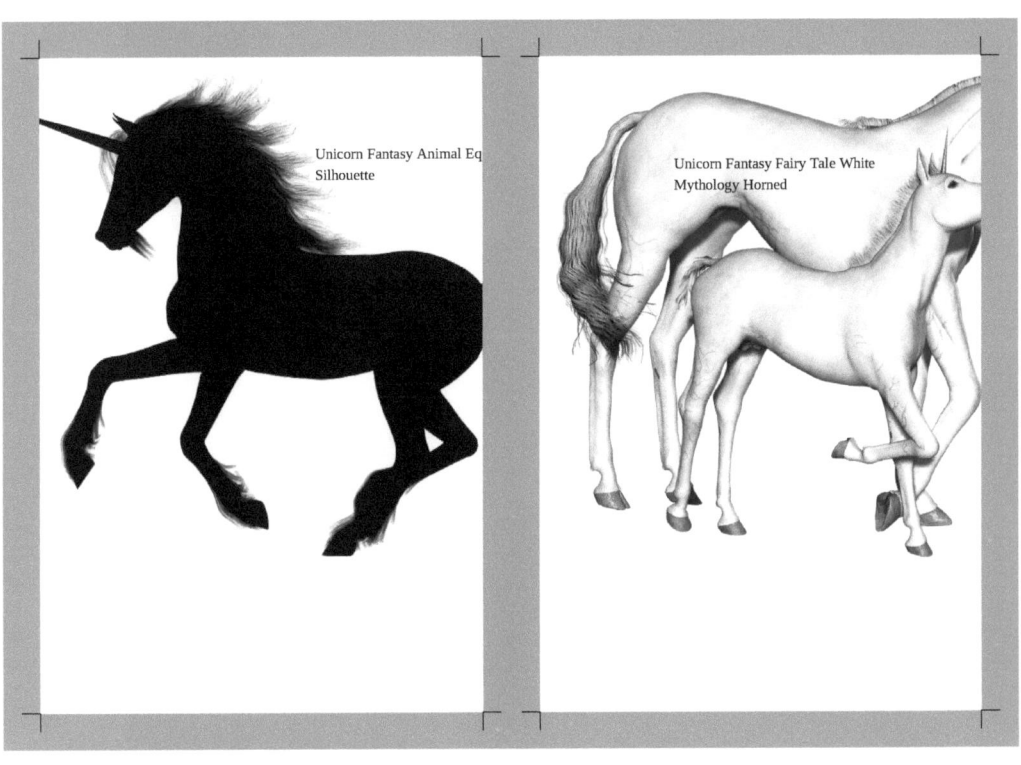

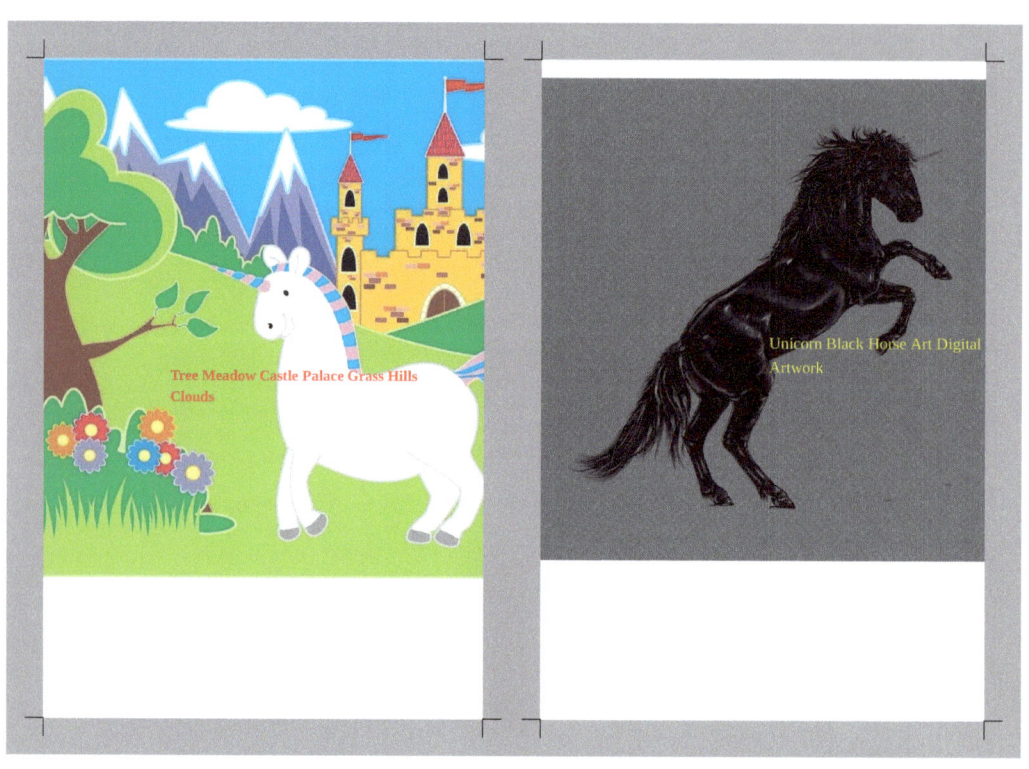

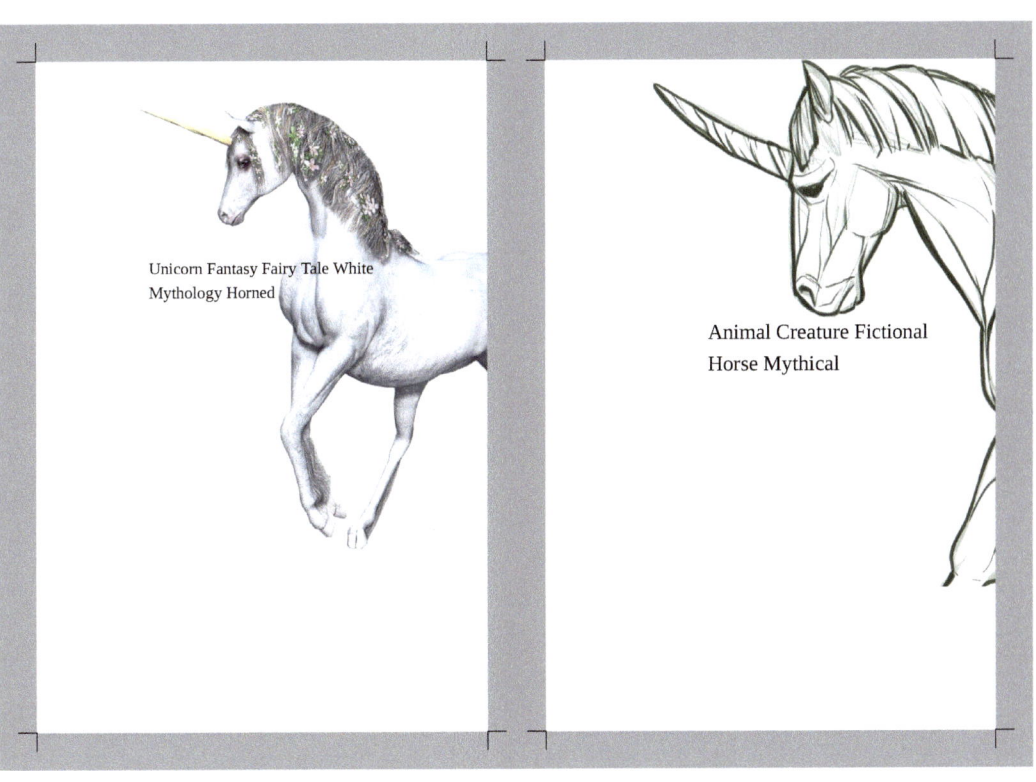

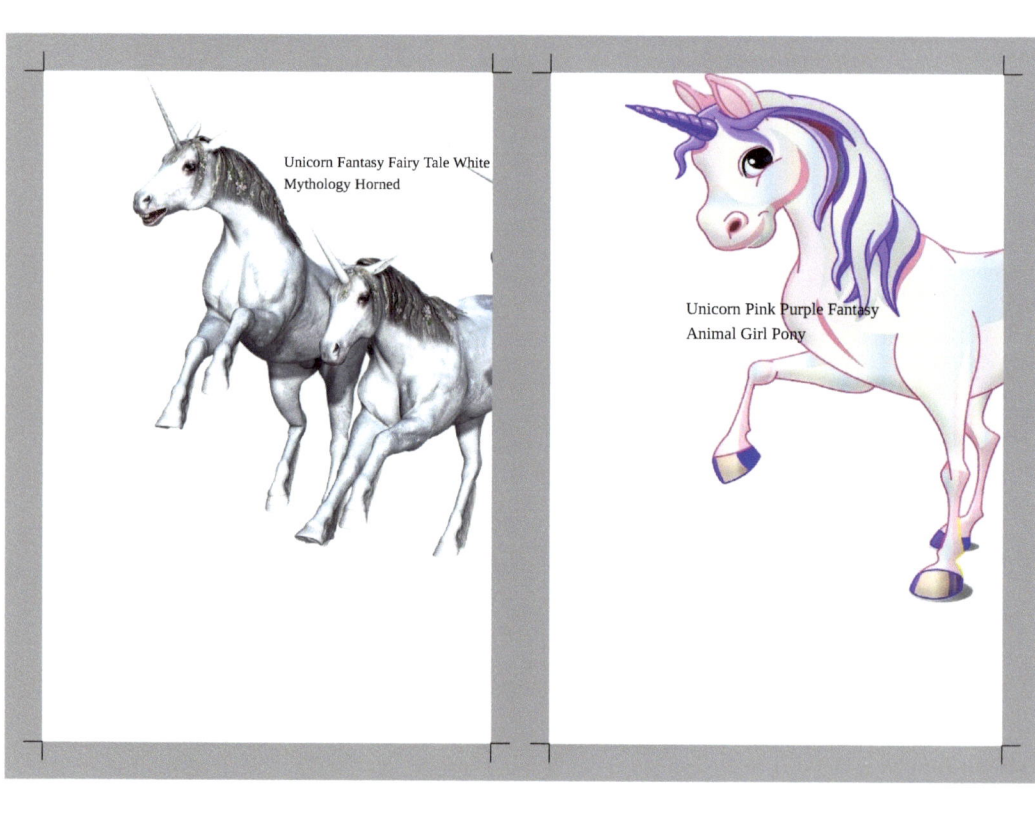

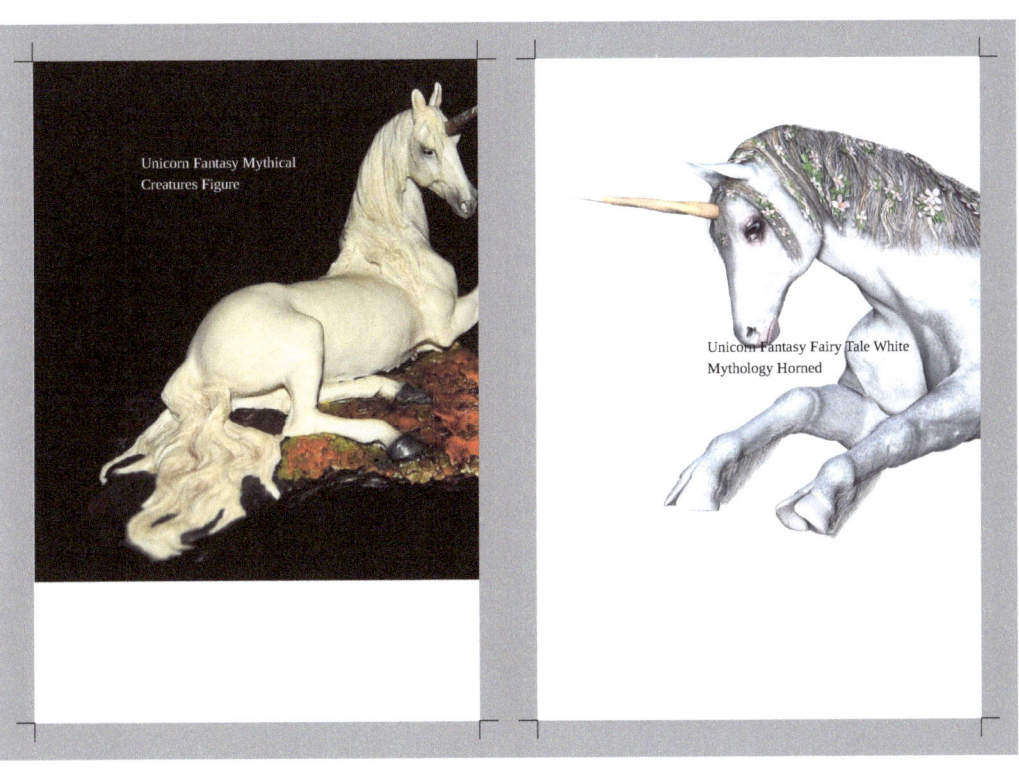

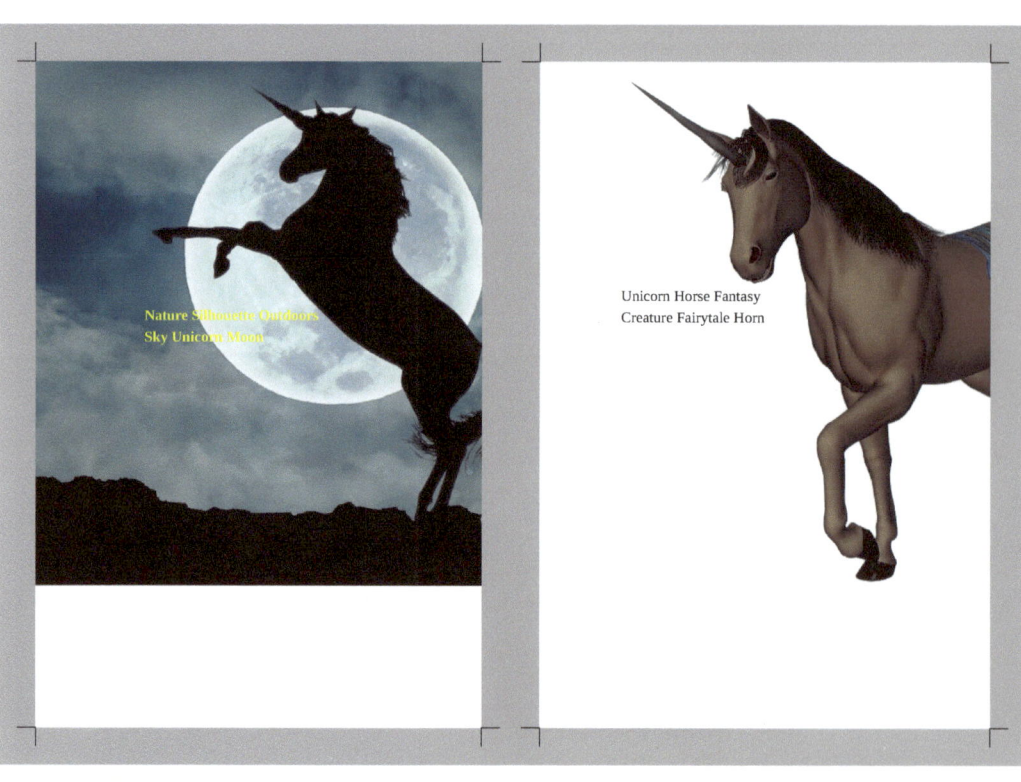

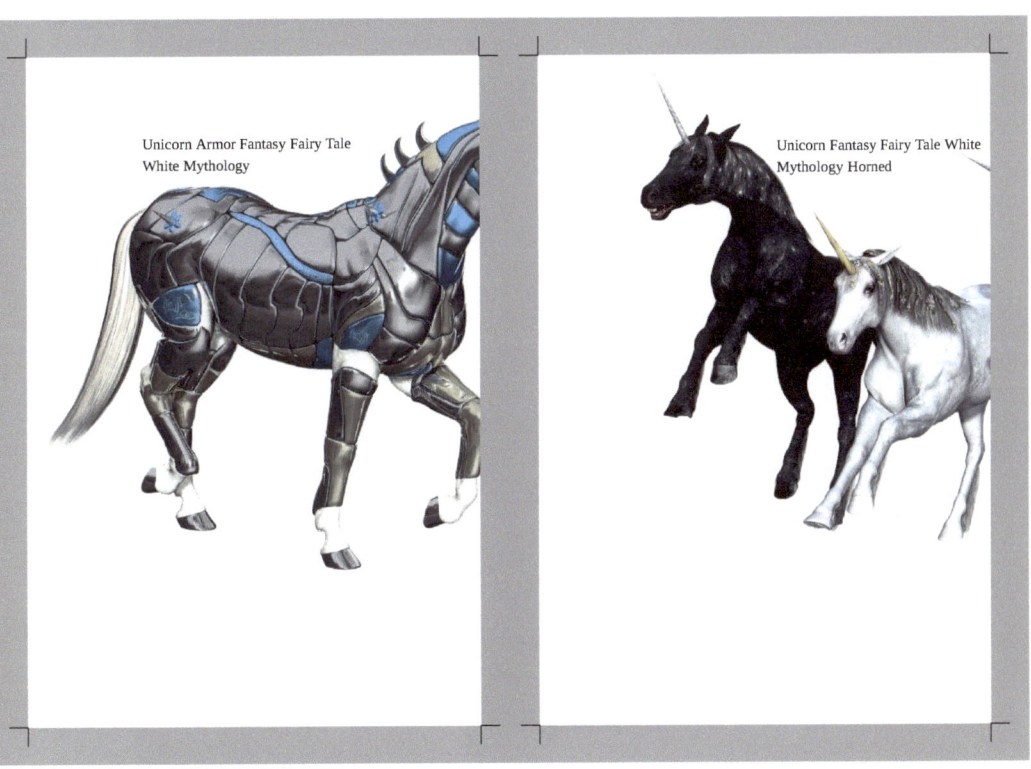

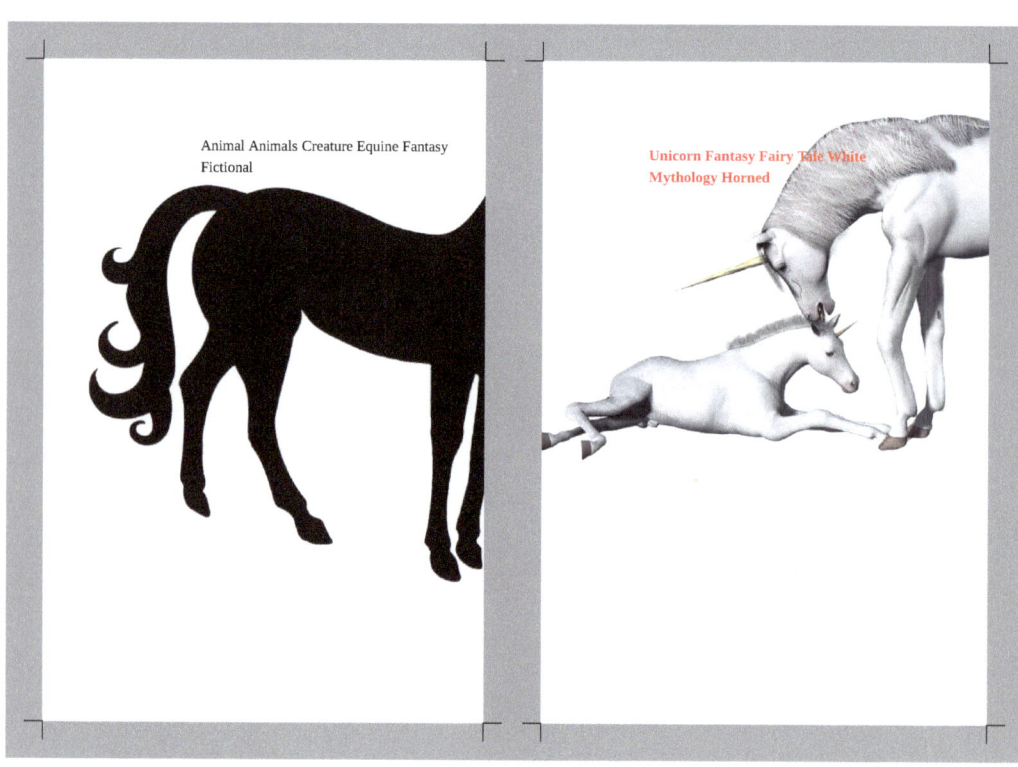

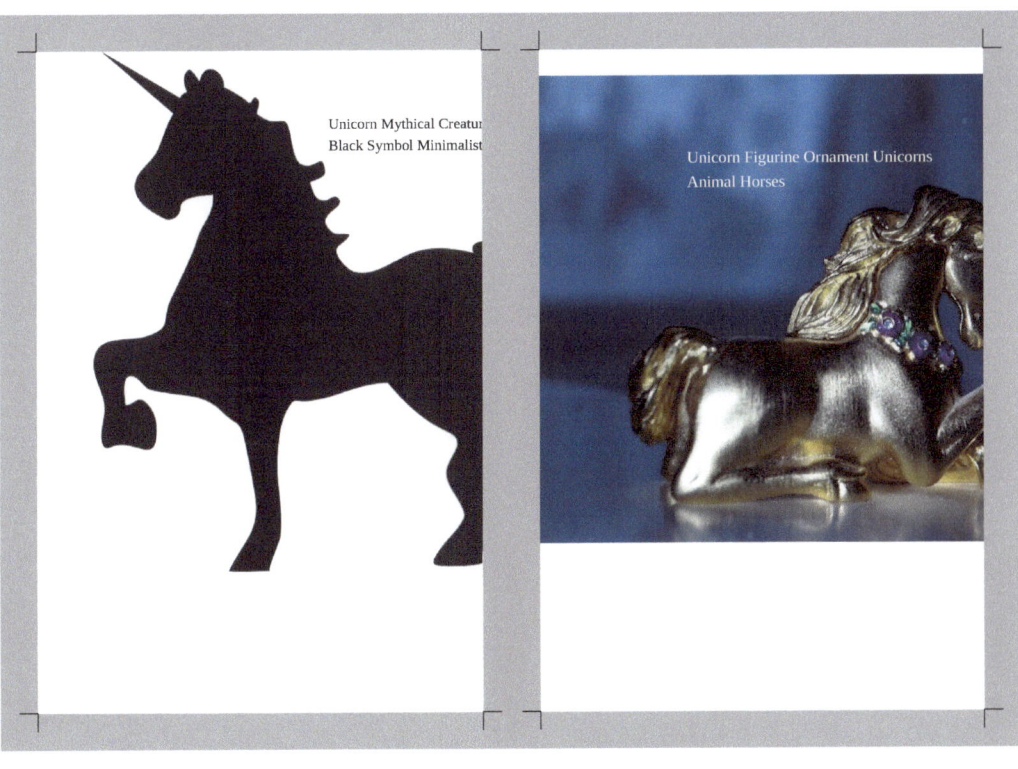

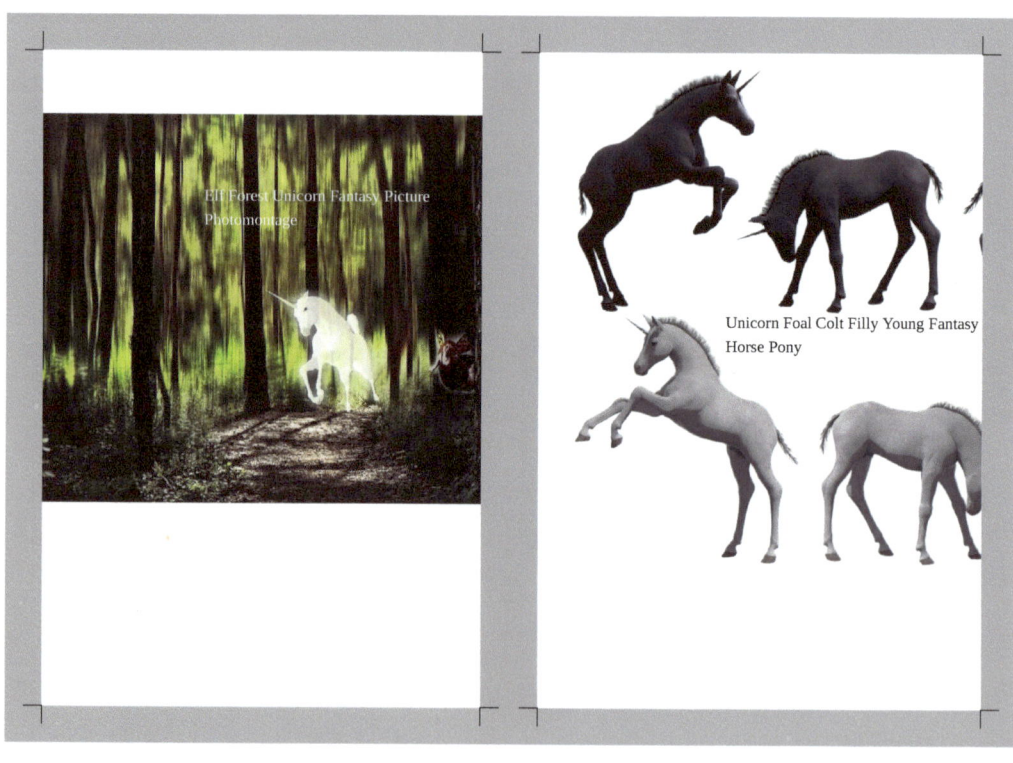

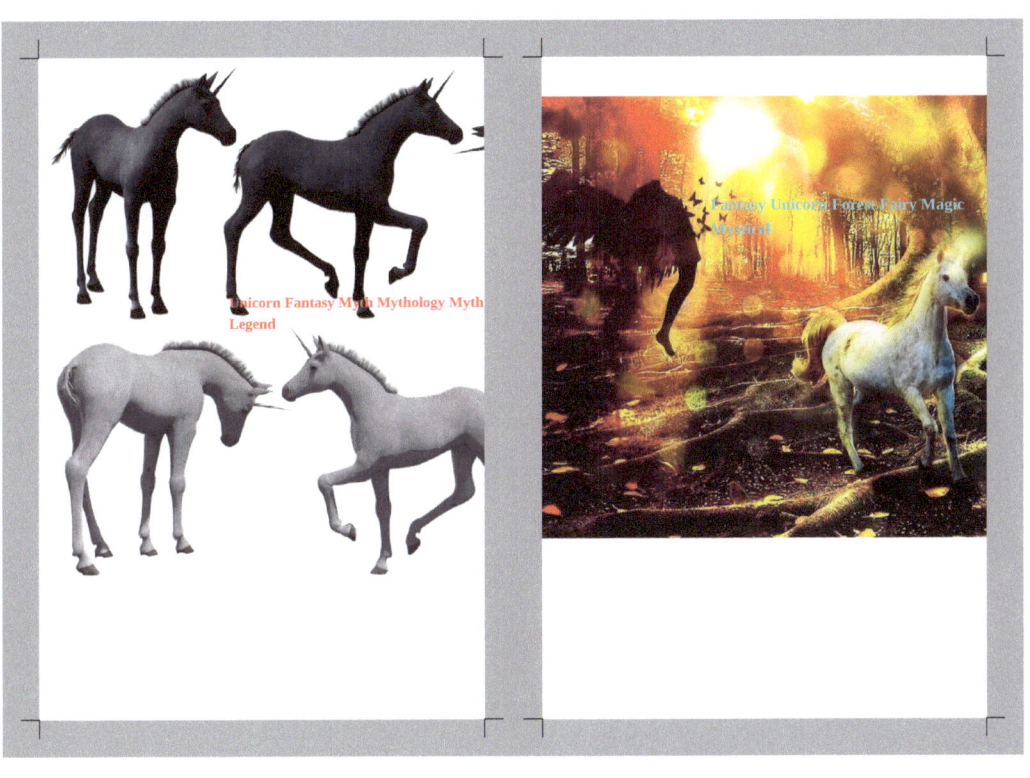

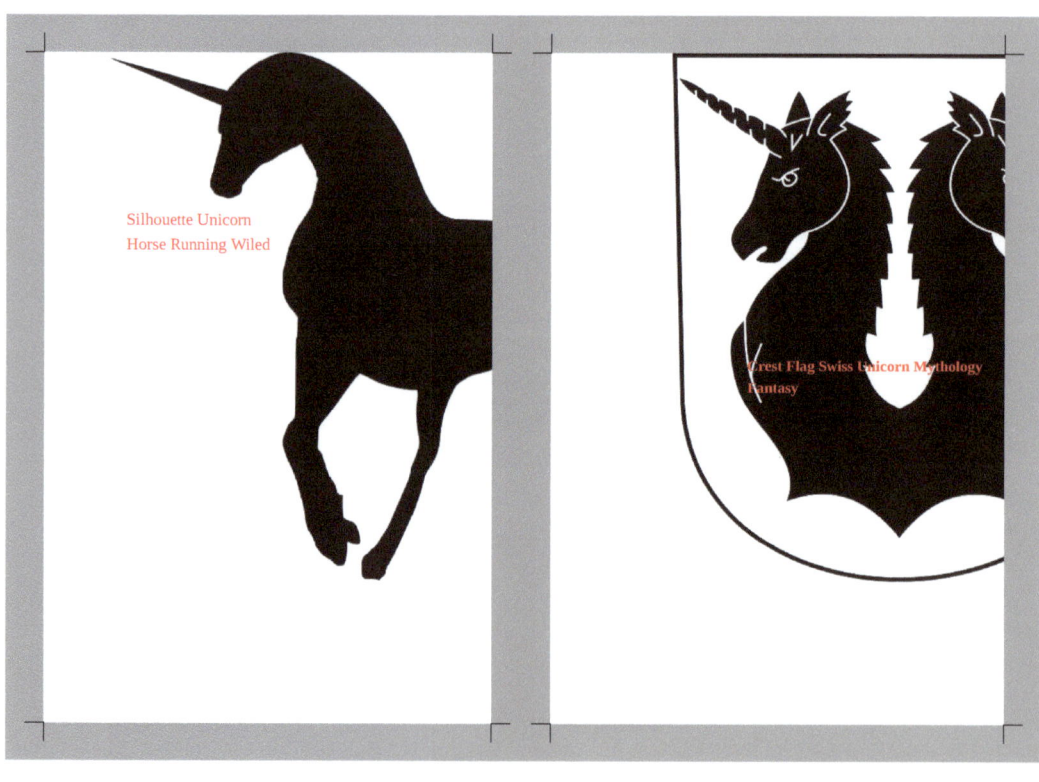

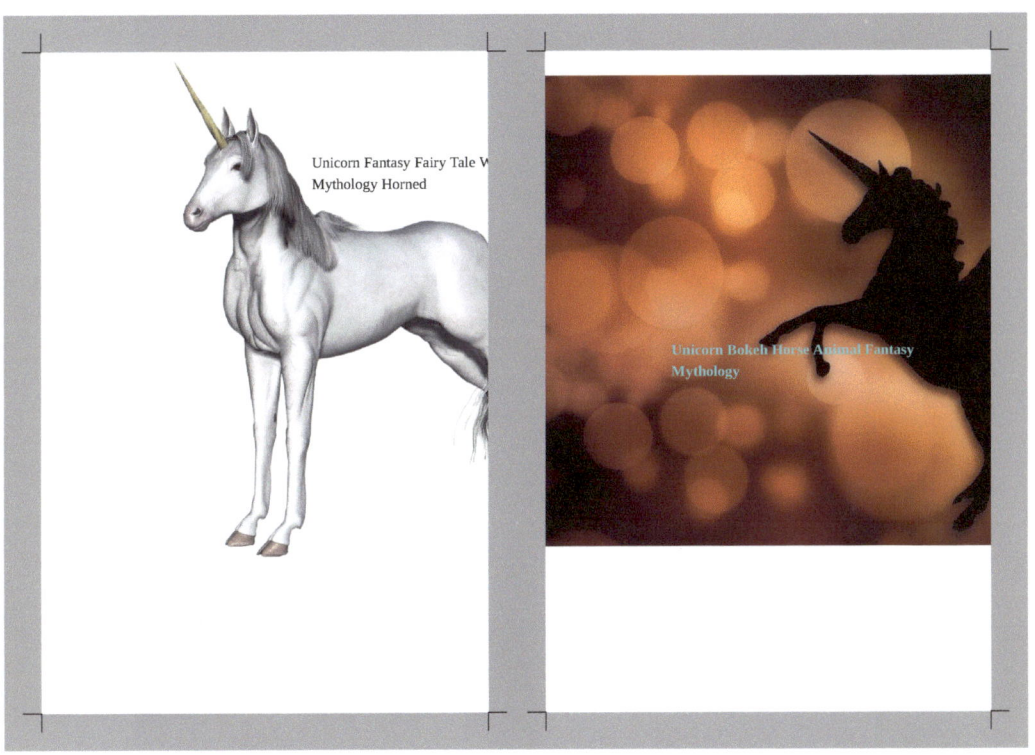

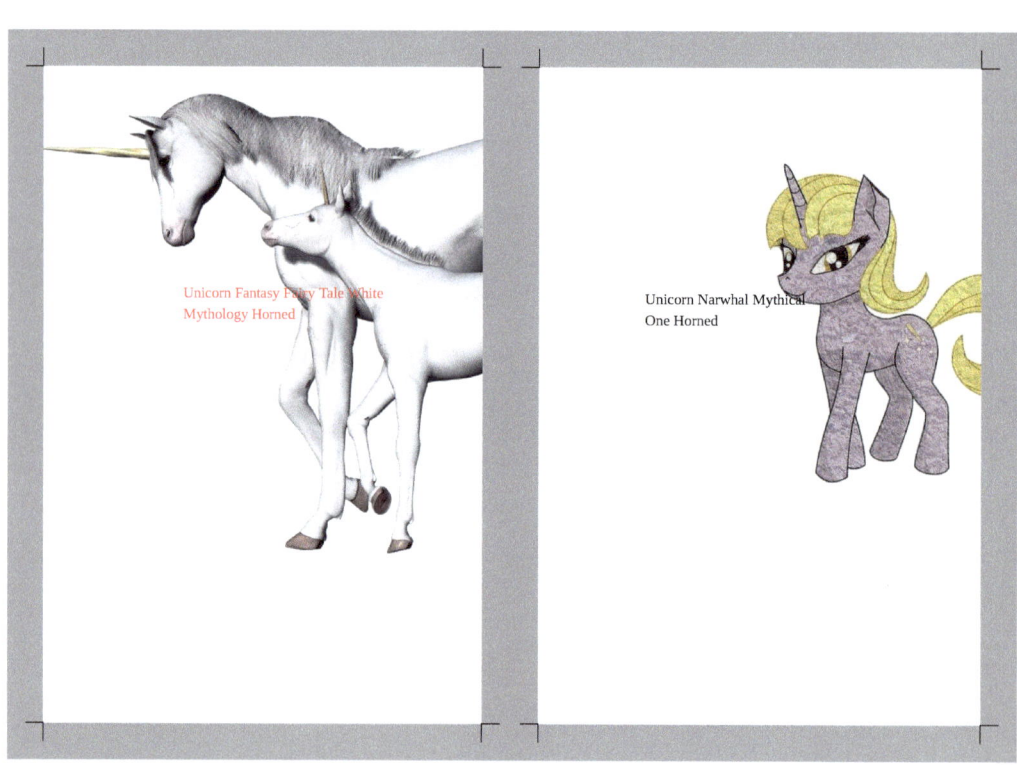

Unicorn Fantasy Fairy Tale White Mythology Horned

Unicorn Narwhal Mythical One Horned

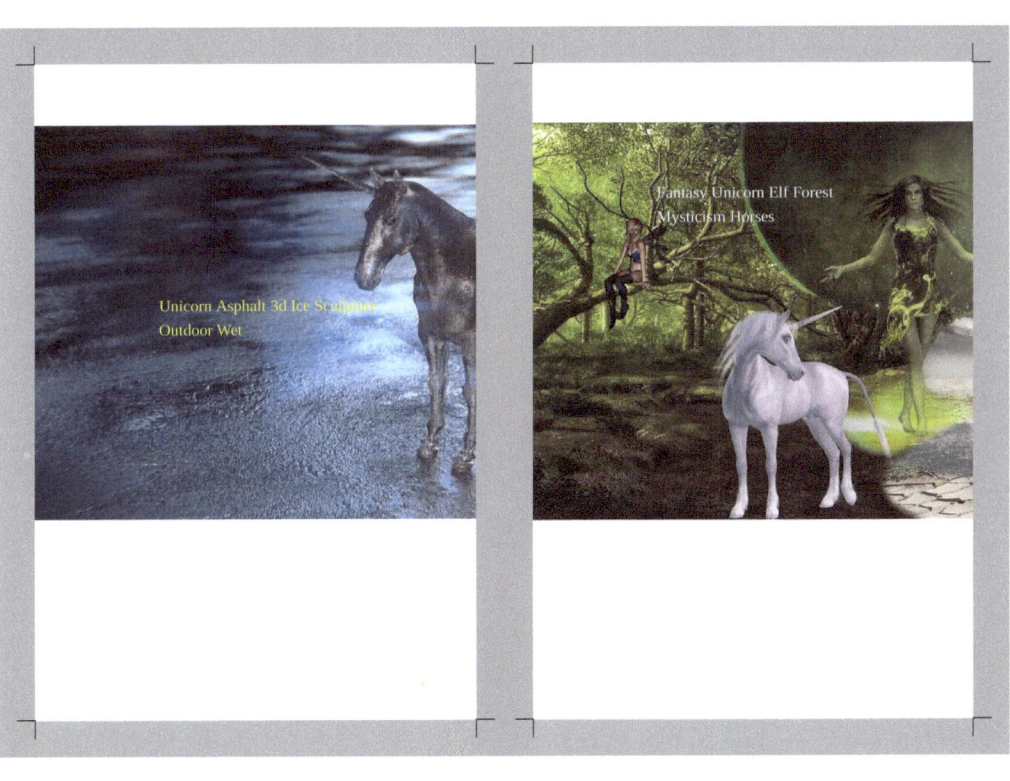

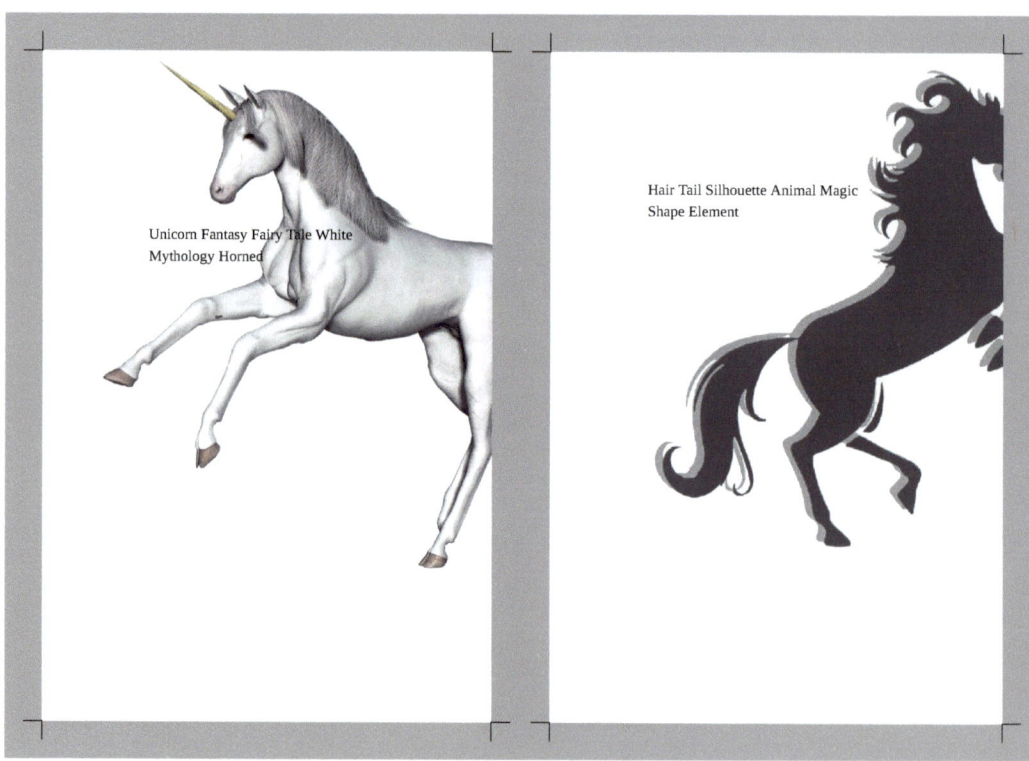

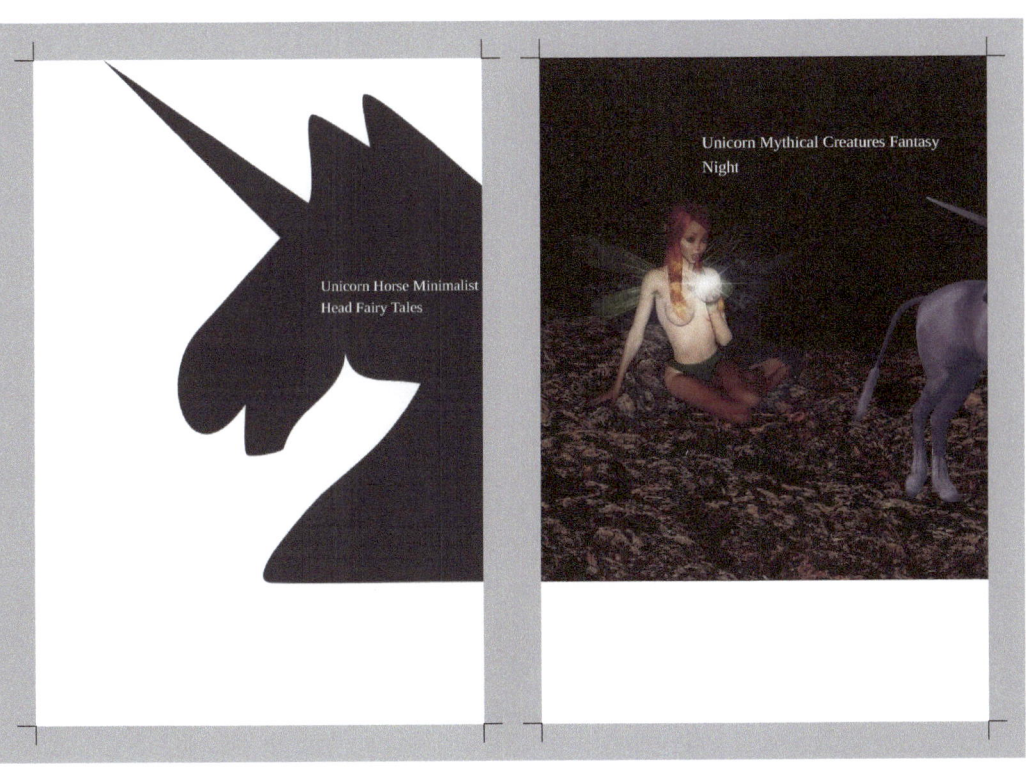

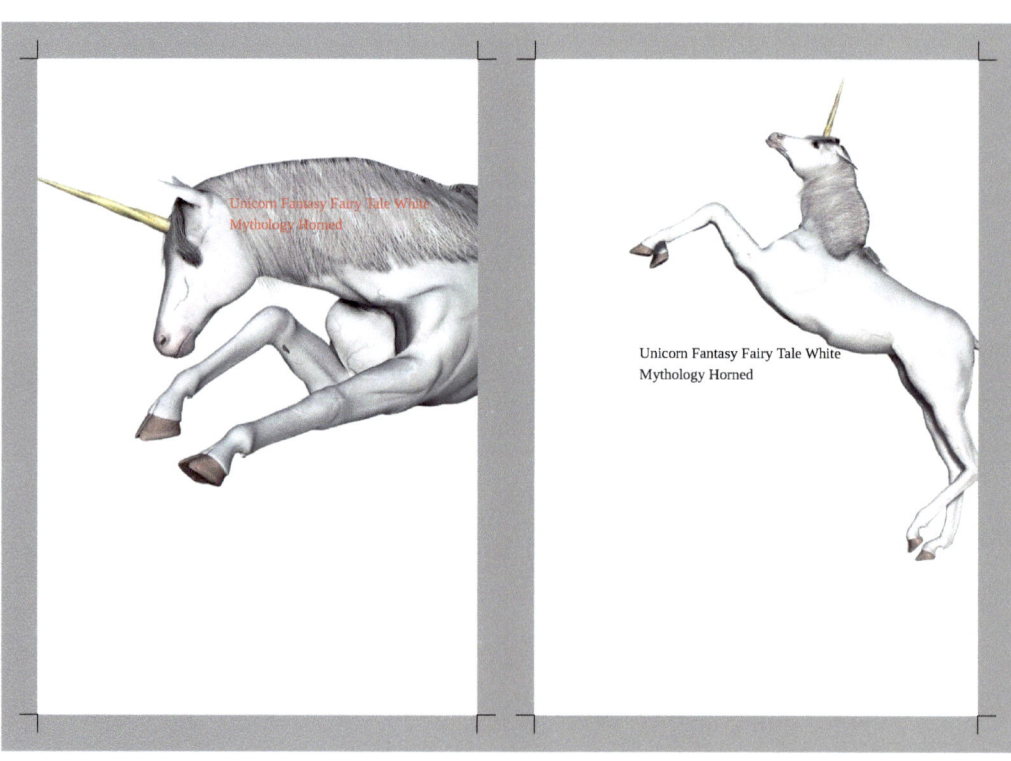

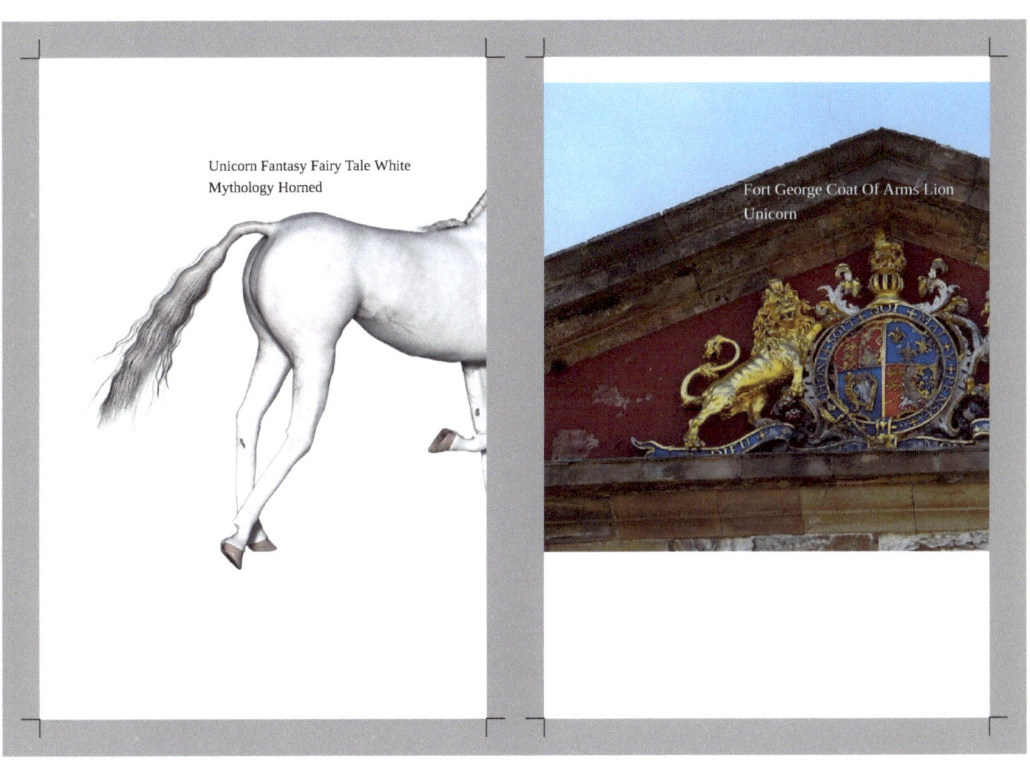

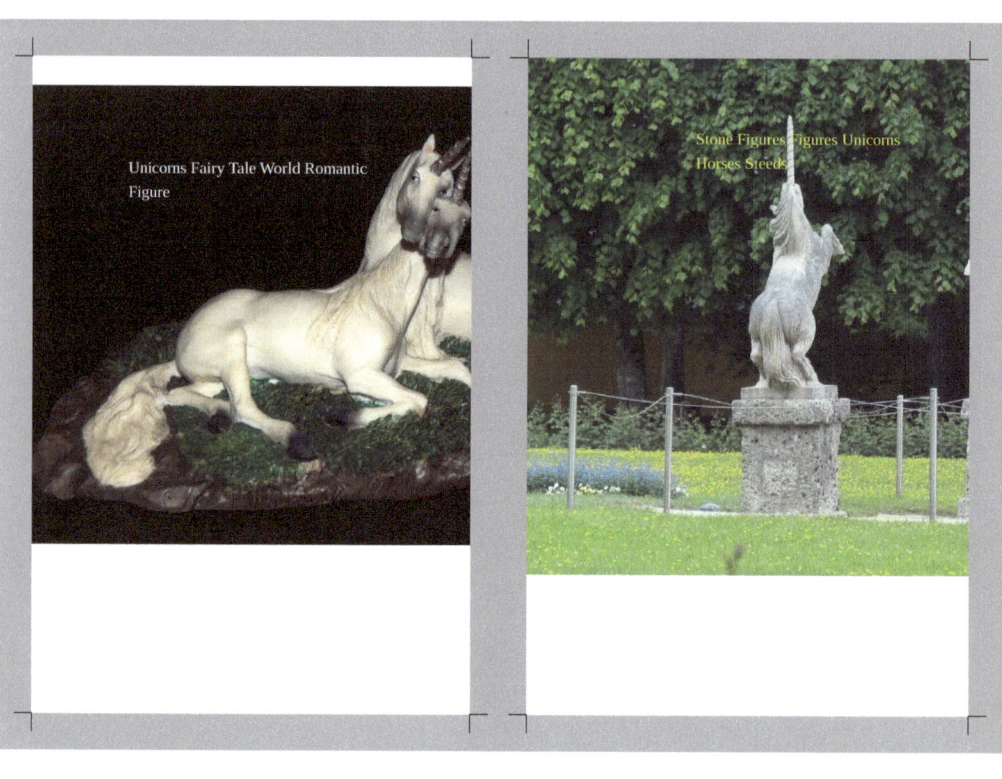

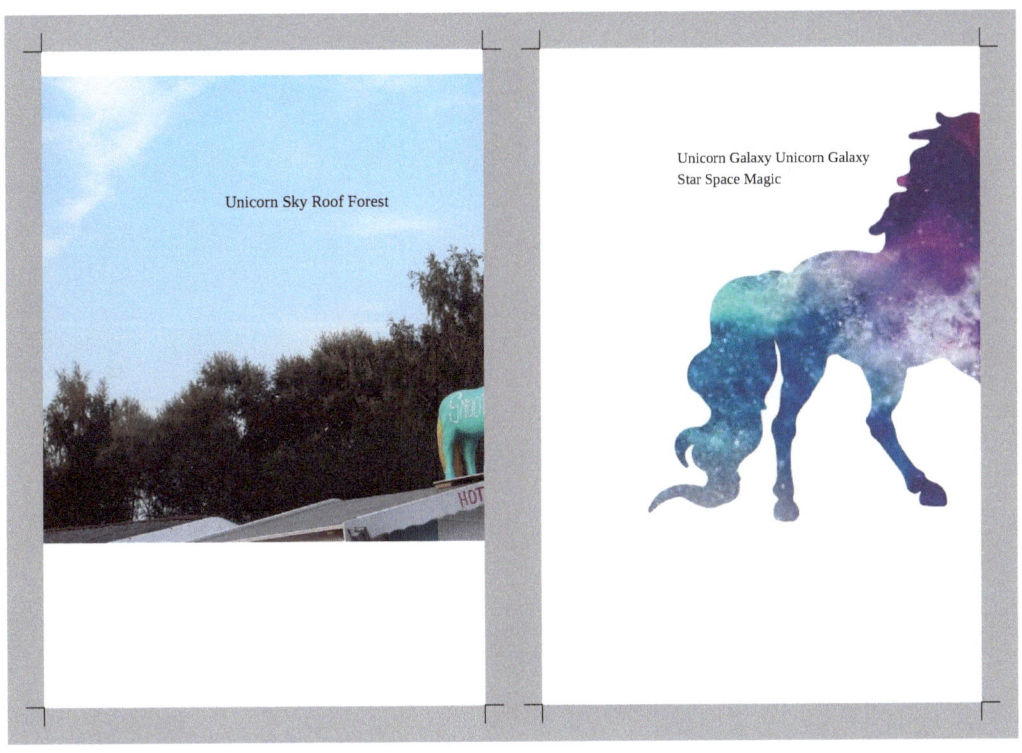

Unicorn Stars Blue Light Phenomenon Color Nature

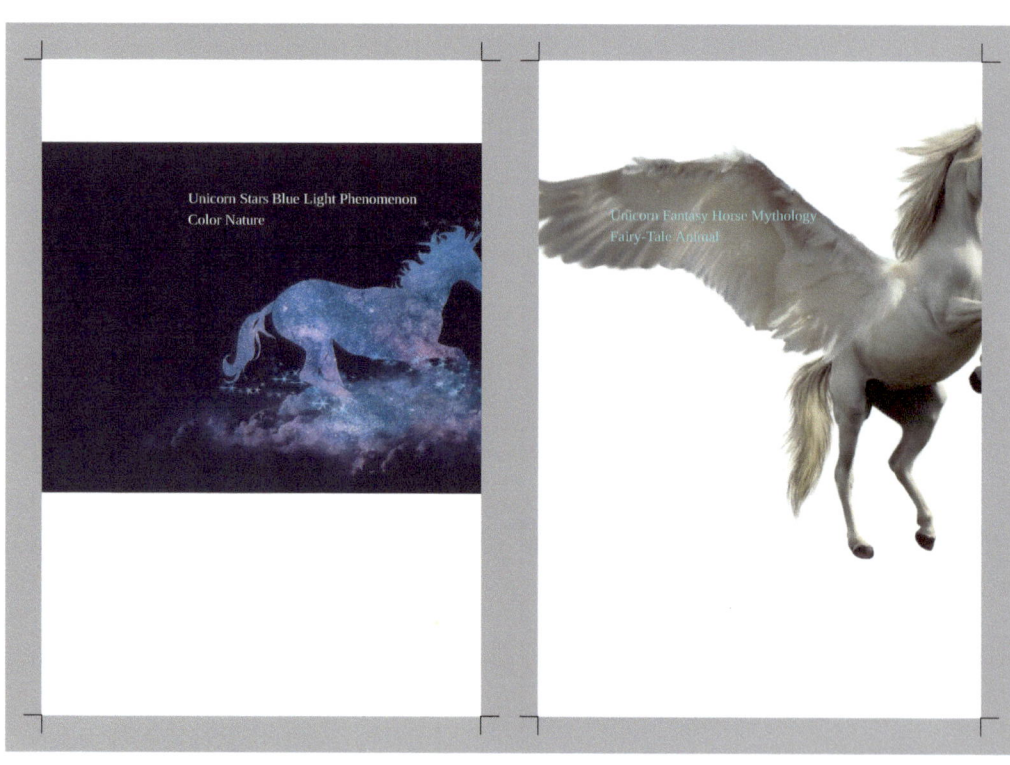

Unicorn Fantasy Horse Mythology Fairy-Tale Animal

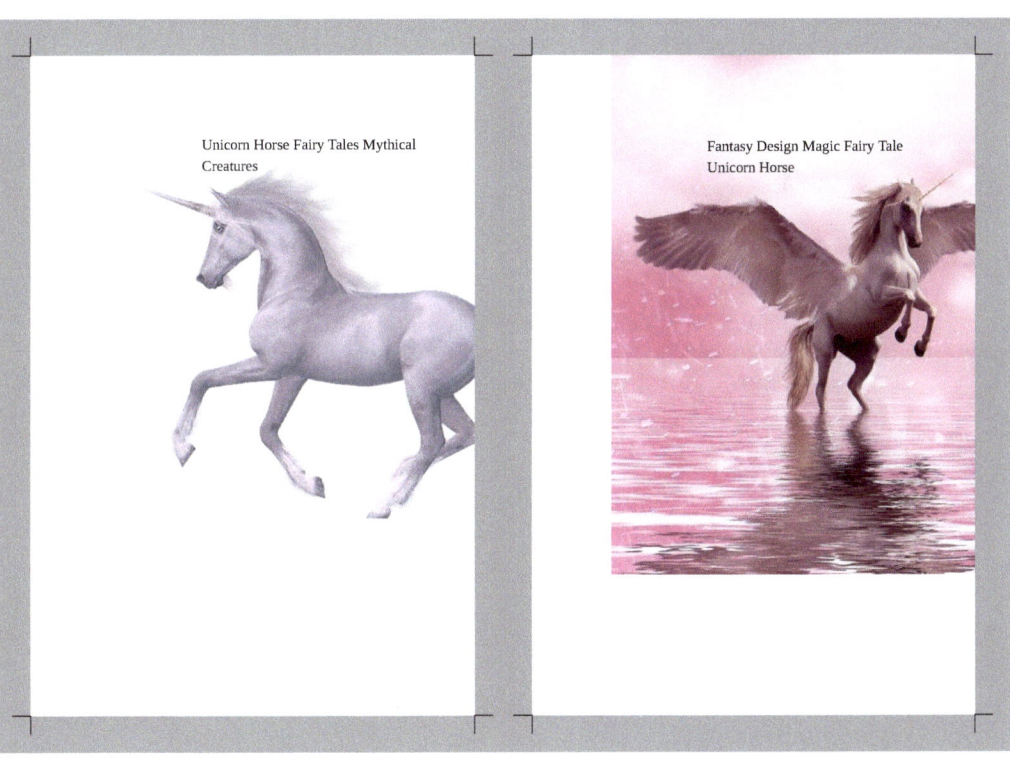

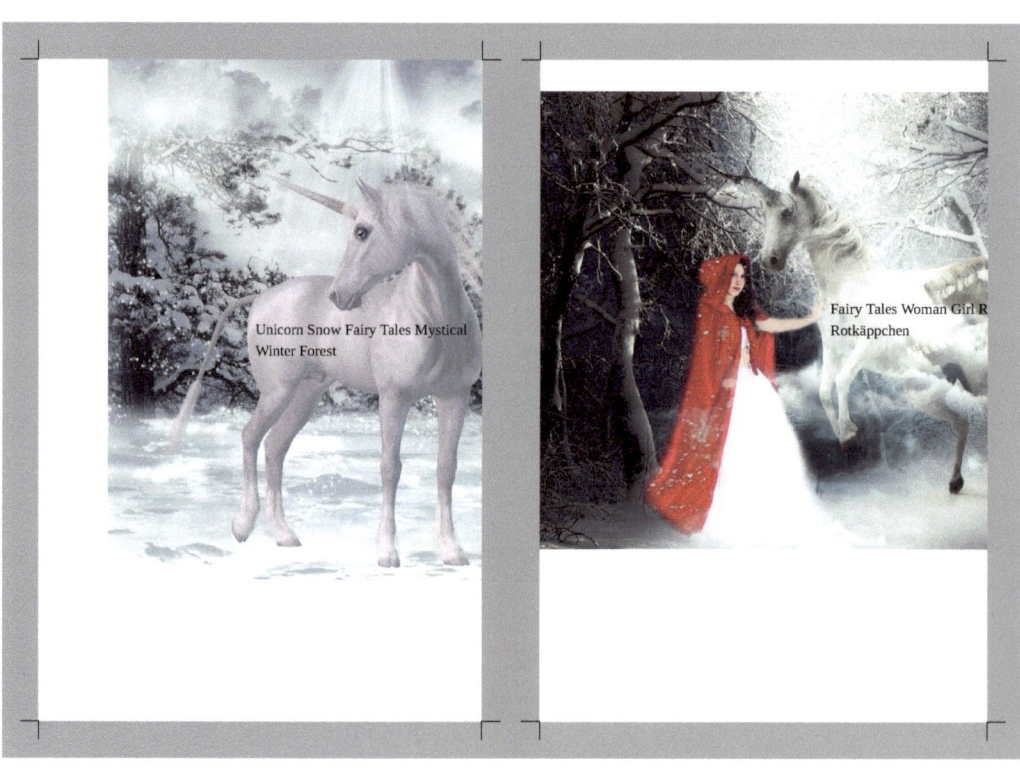

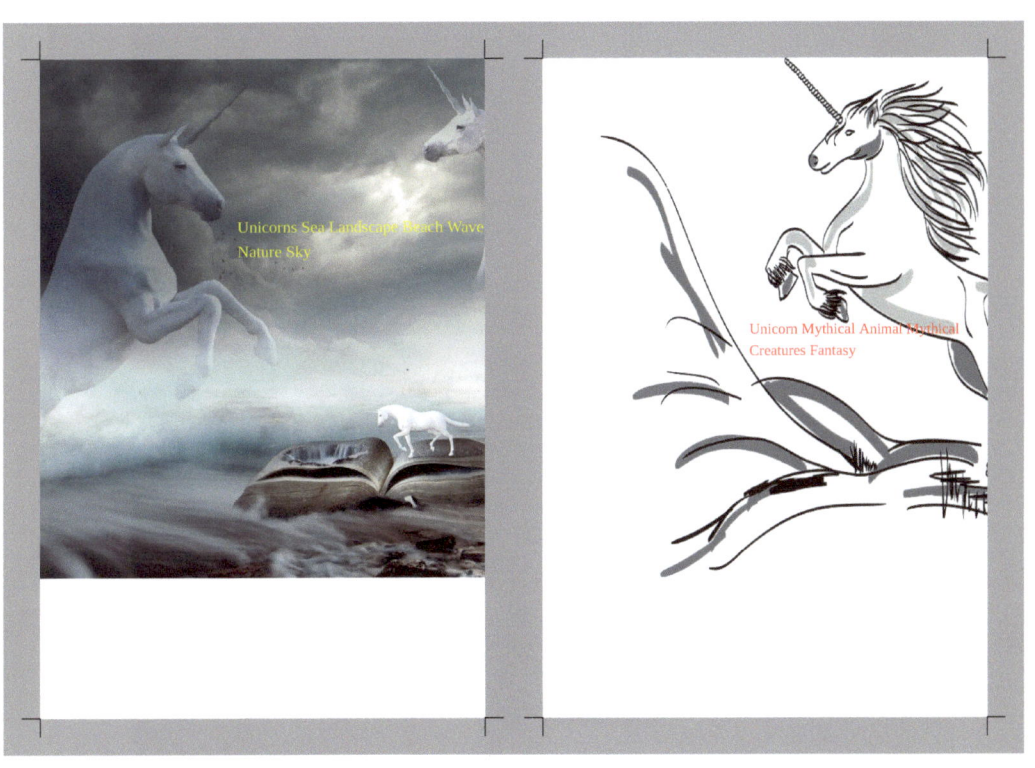

Unicorn Horse Flower Florist Narwhal Mythical

Unicorn Galaxy Fantasy Star Space Cosmic Planet

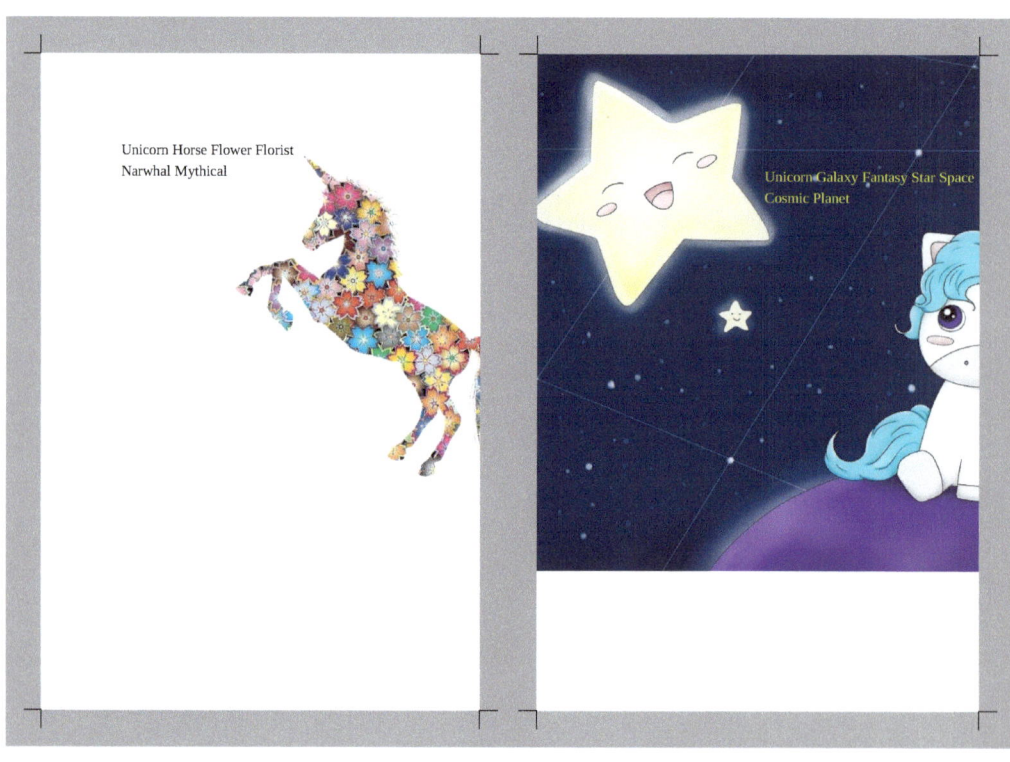

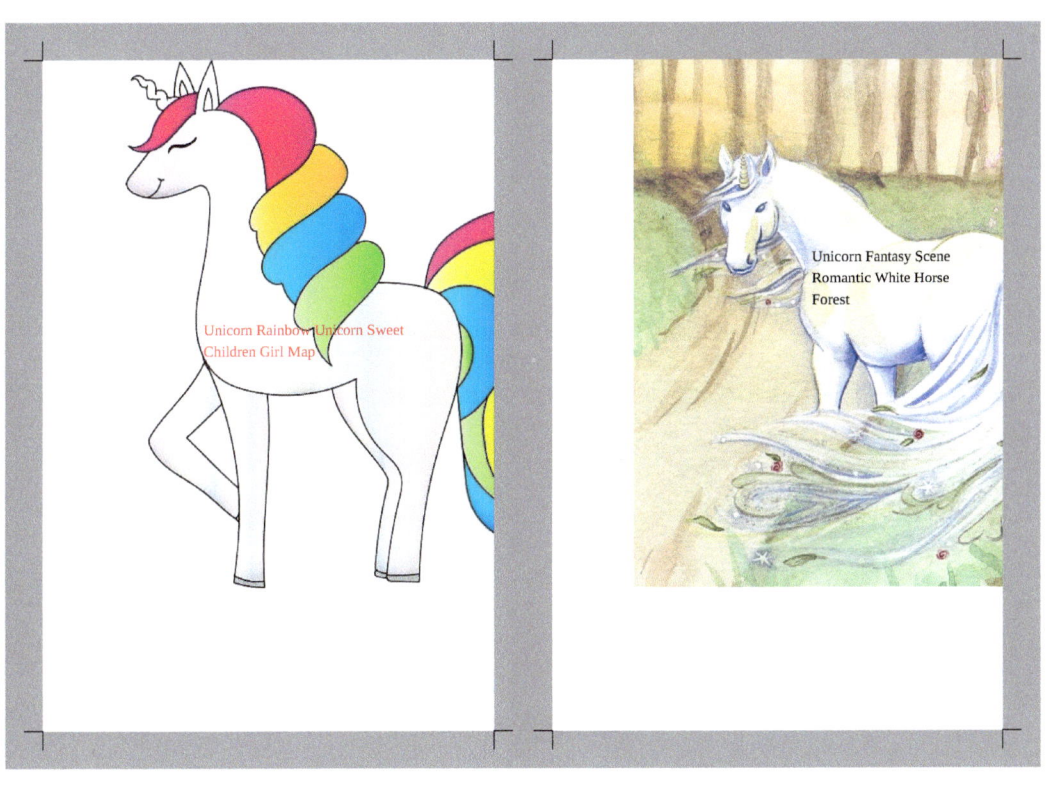

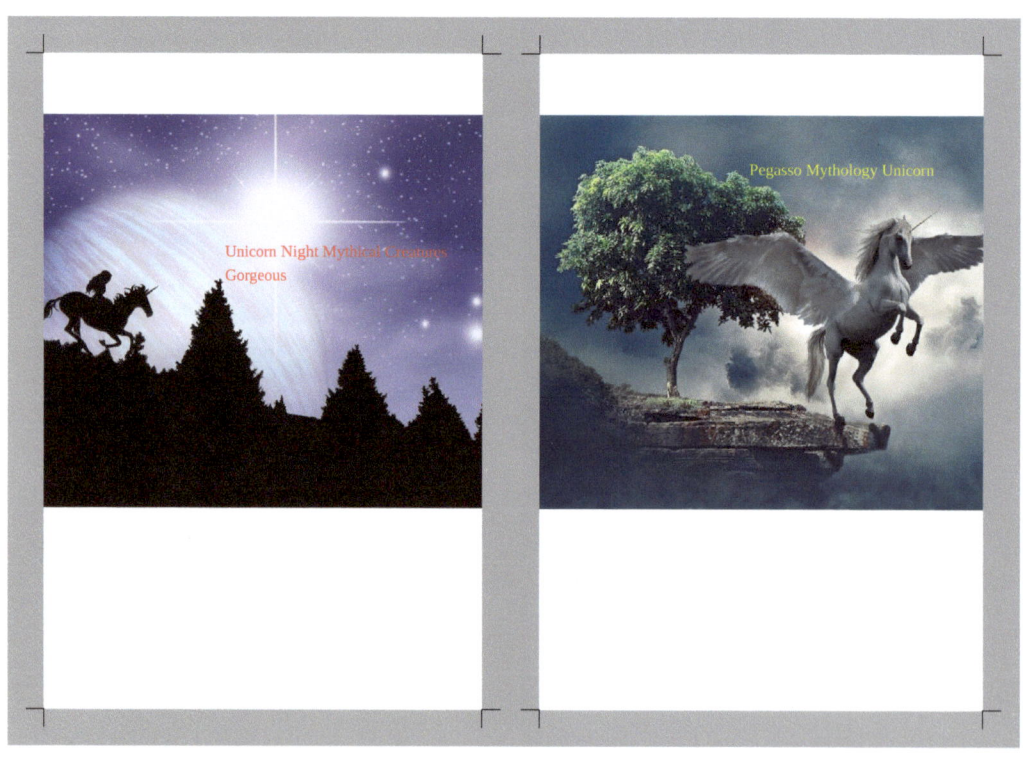

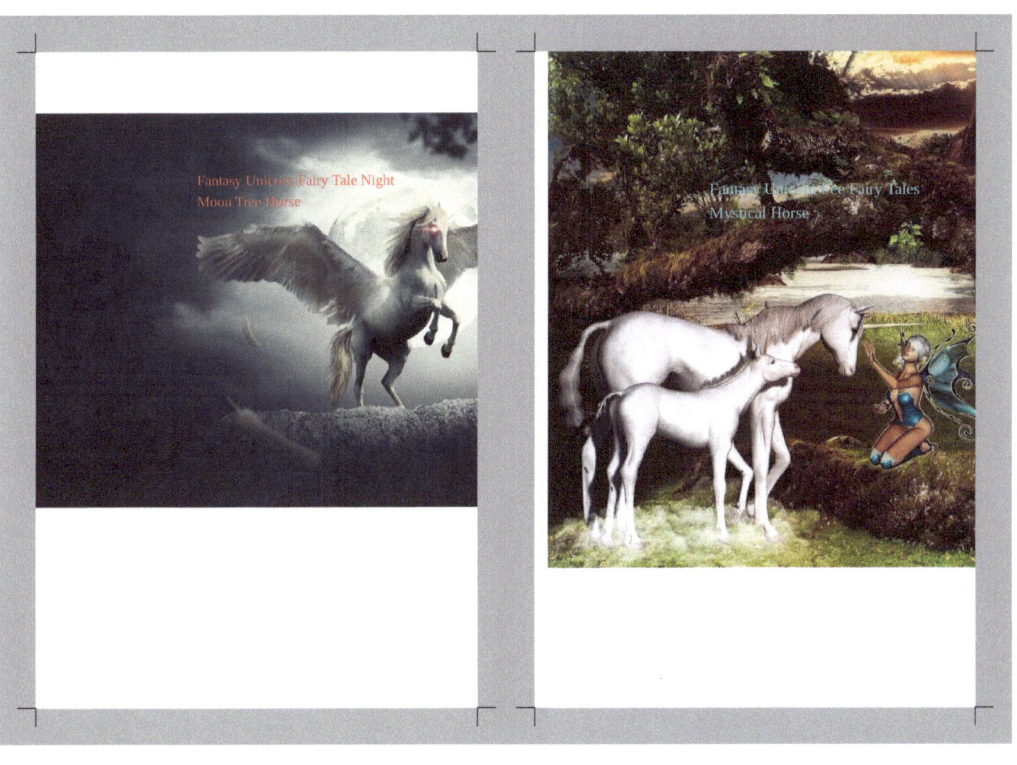

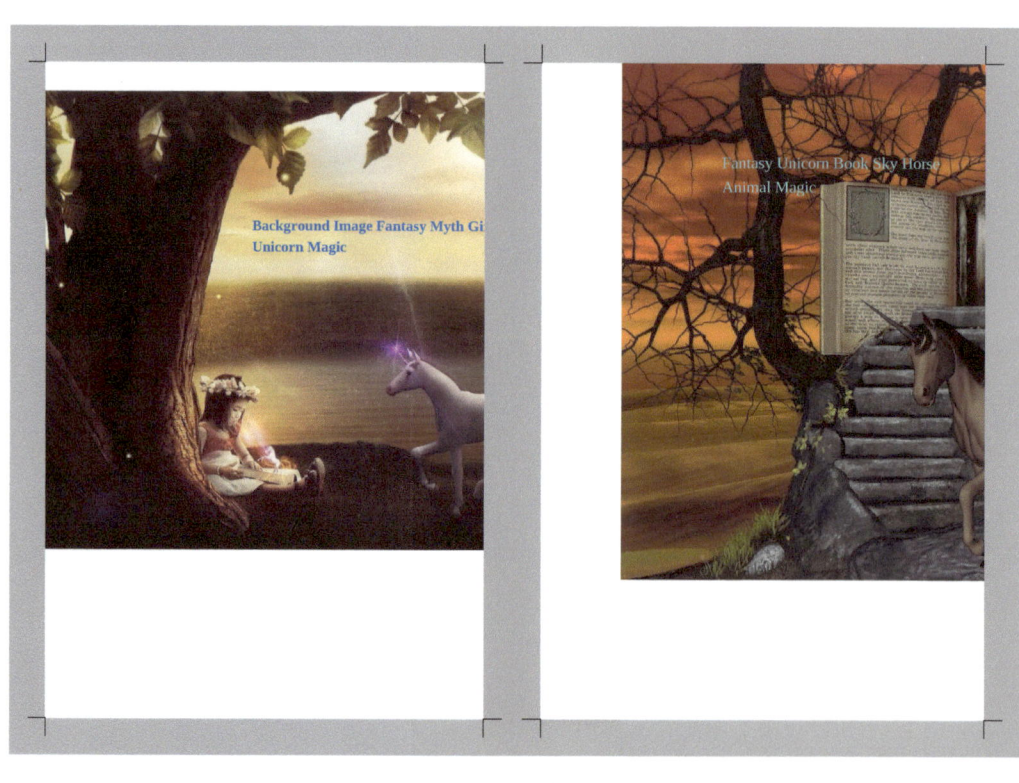

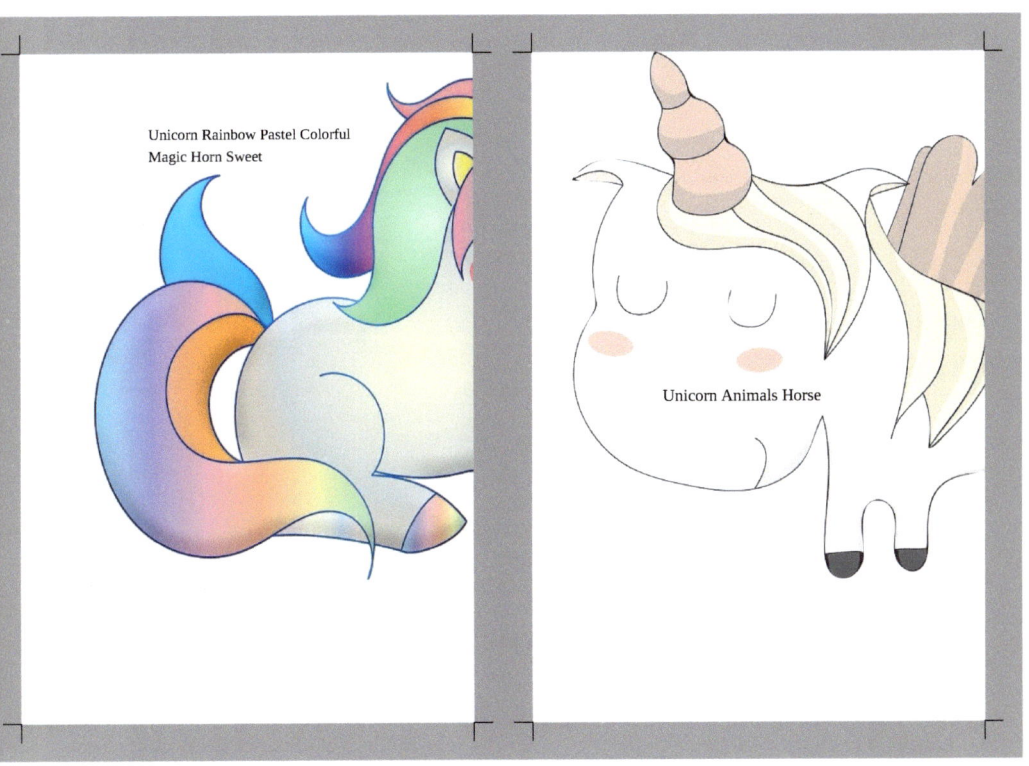

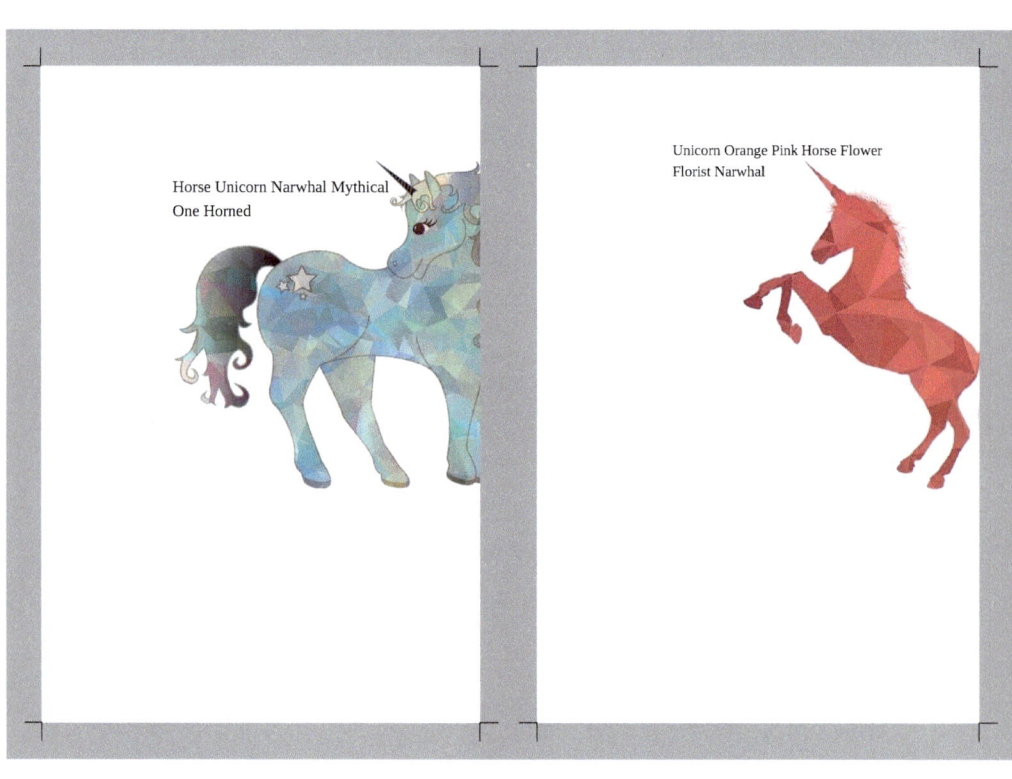

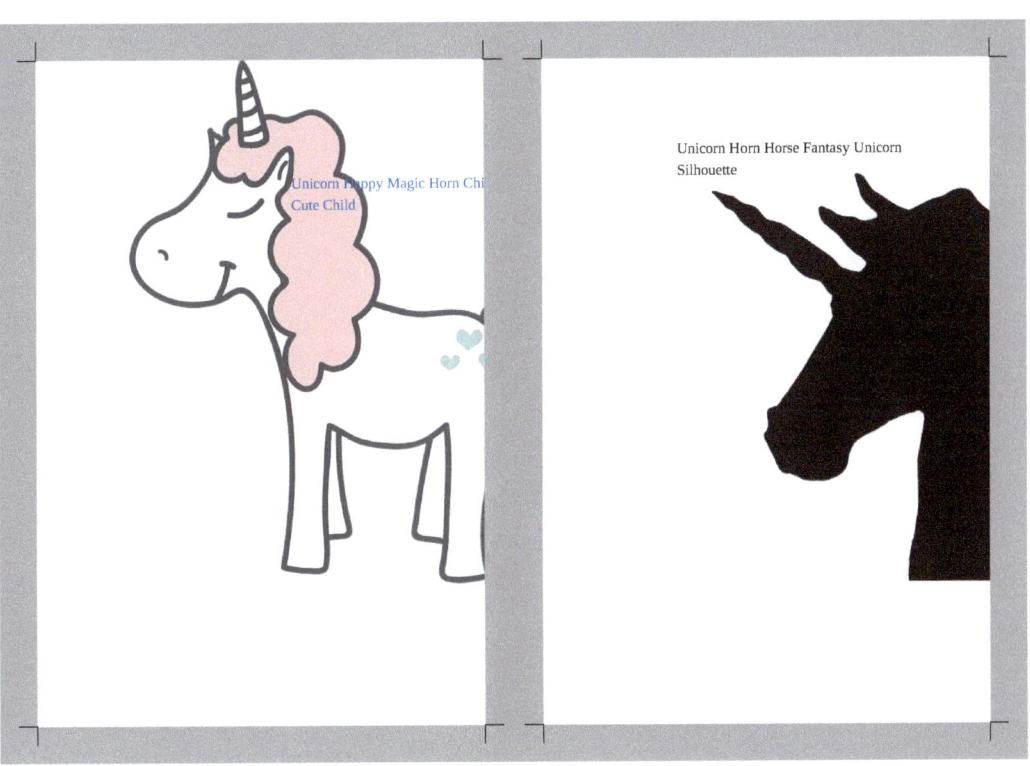

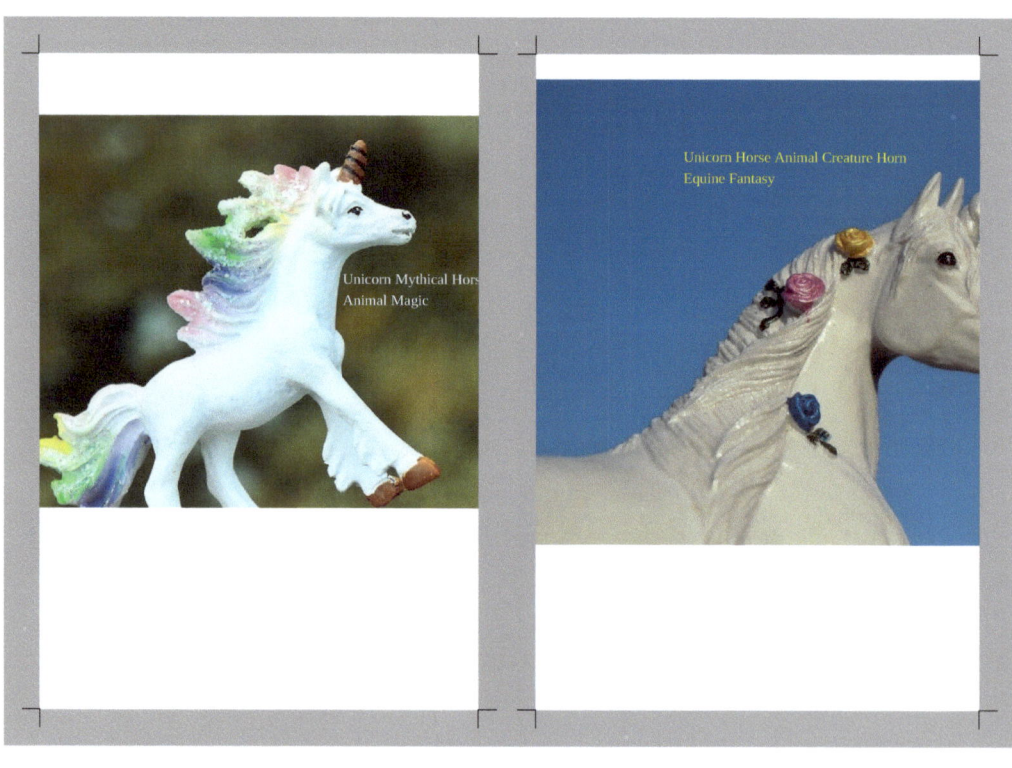

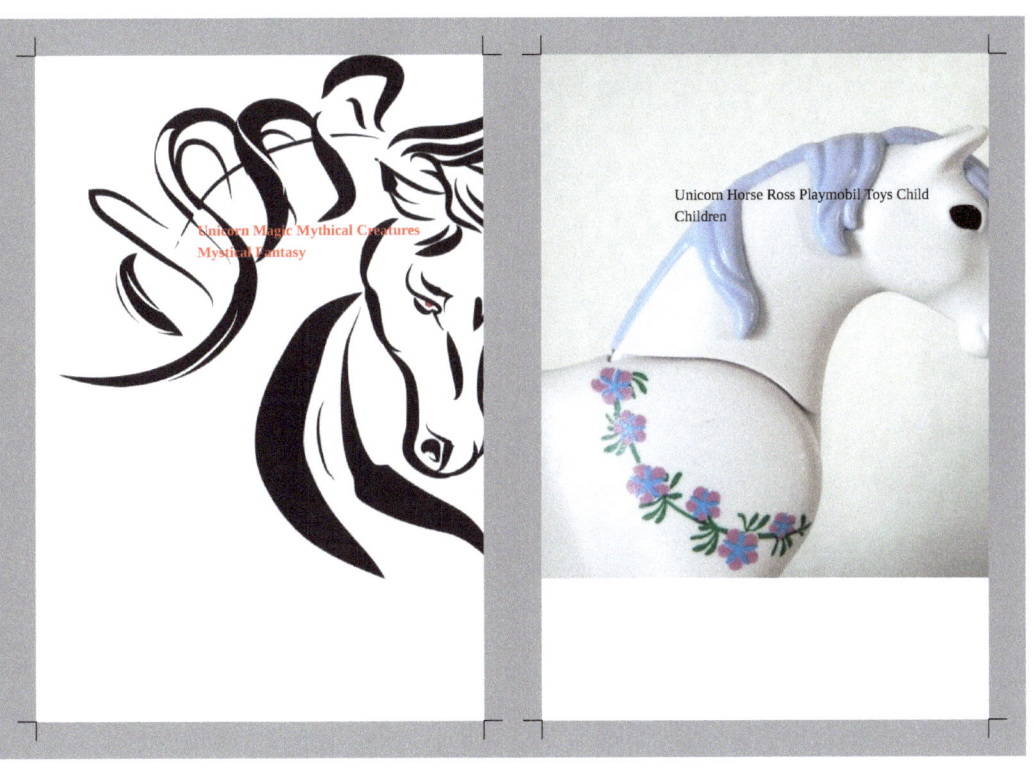

Unicorn Magic Mythical Creatures Mystical Fantasy

Unicorn Horse Ross Playmobil Toys Child Children

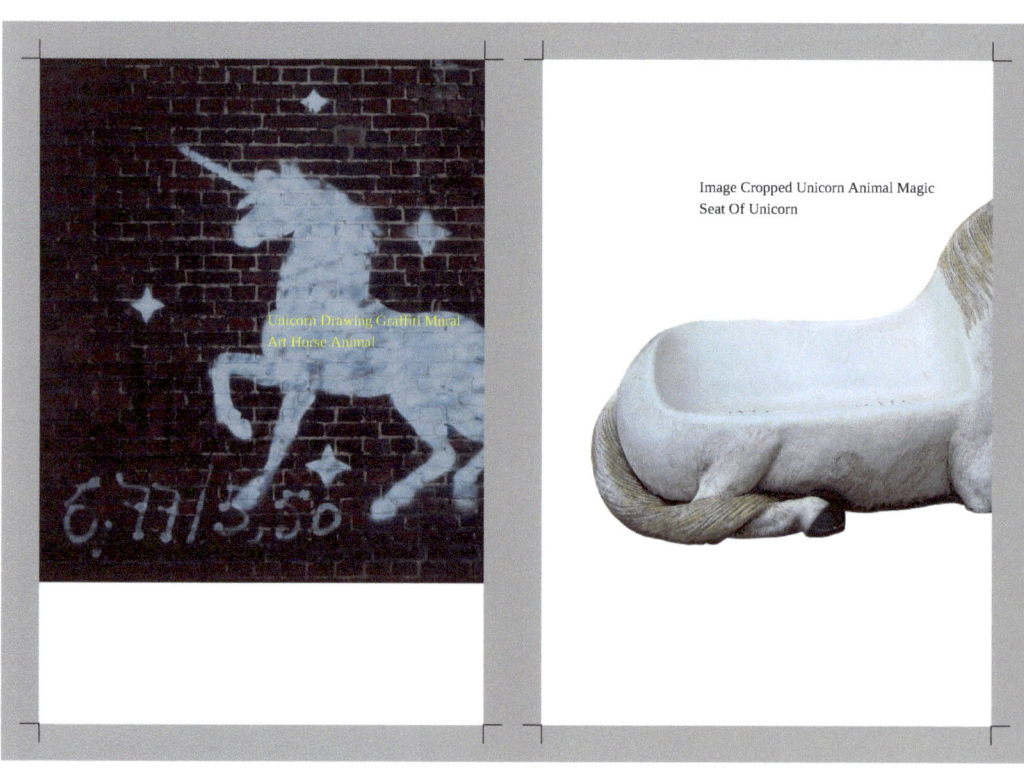

Unicorn Drawing Graffiti Mural Art Horse Animal

Image Cropped Unicorn Animal Magic Seat Of Unicorn

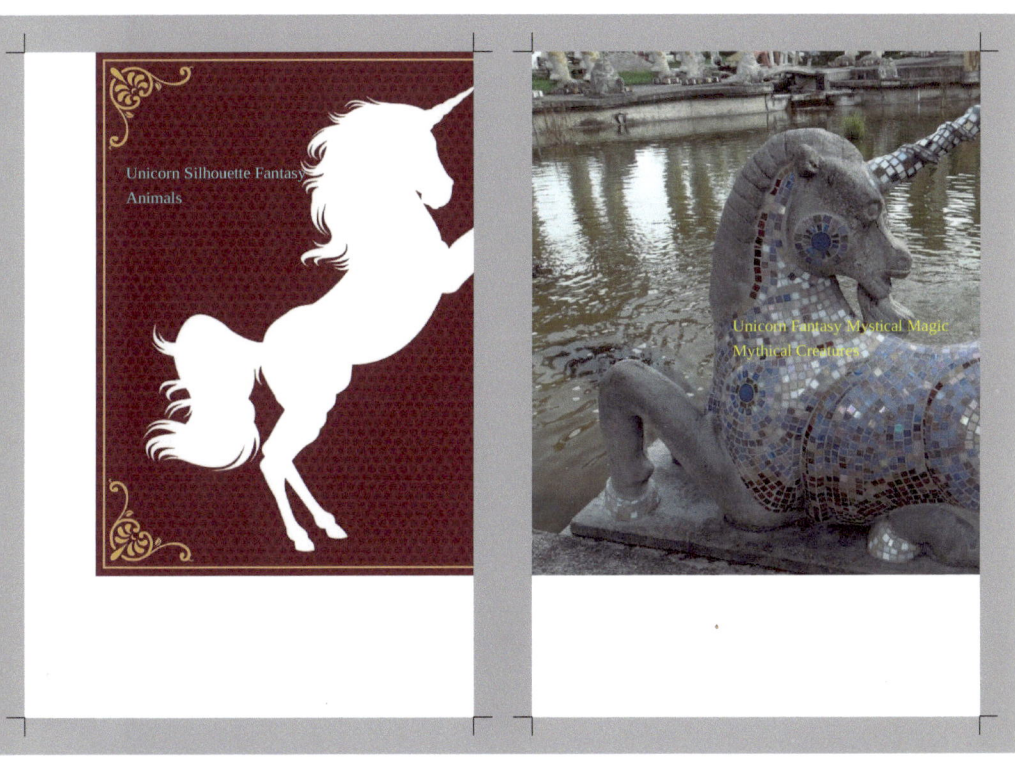

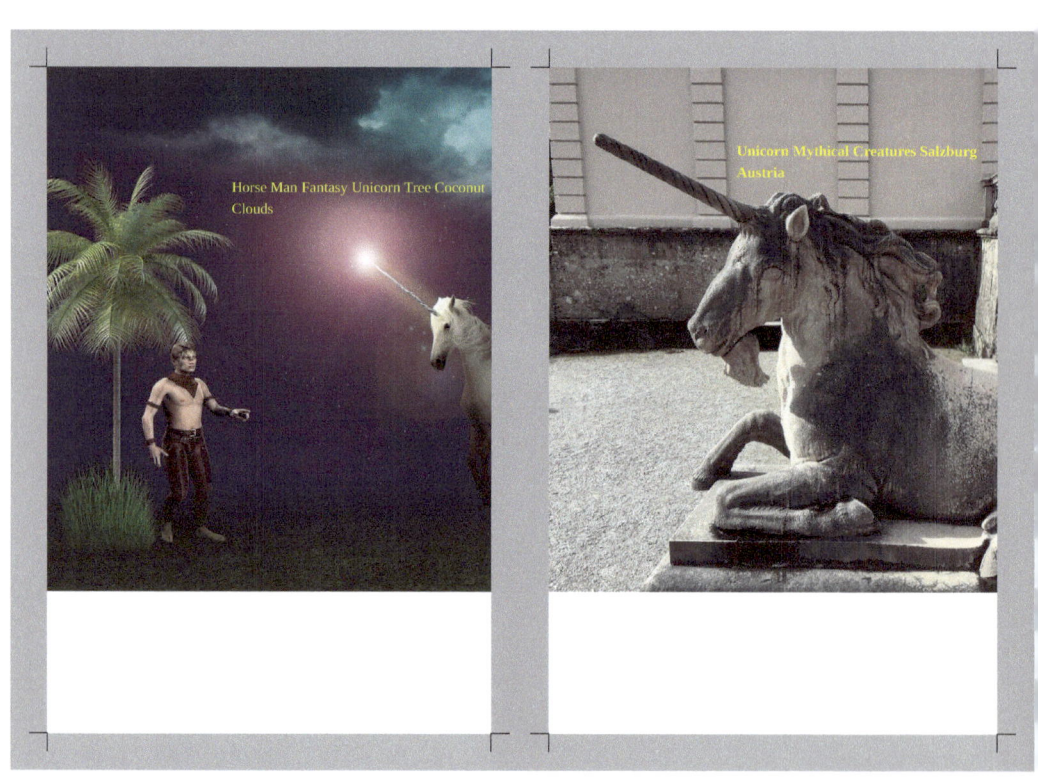

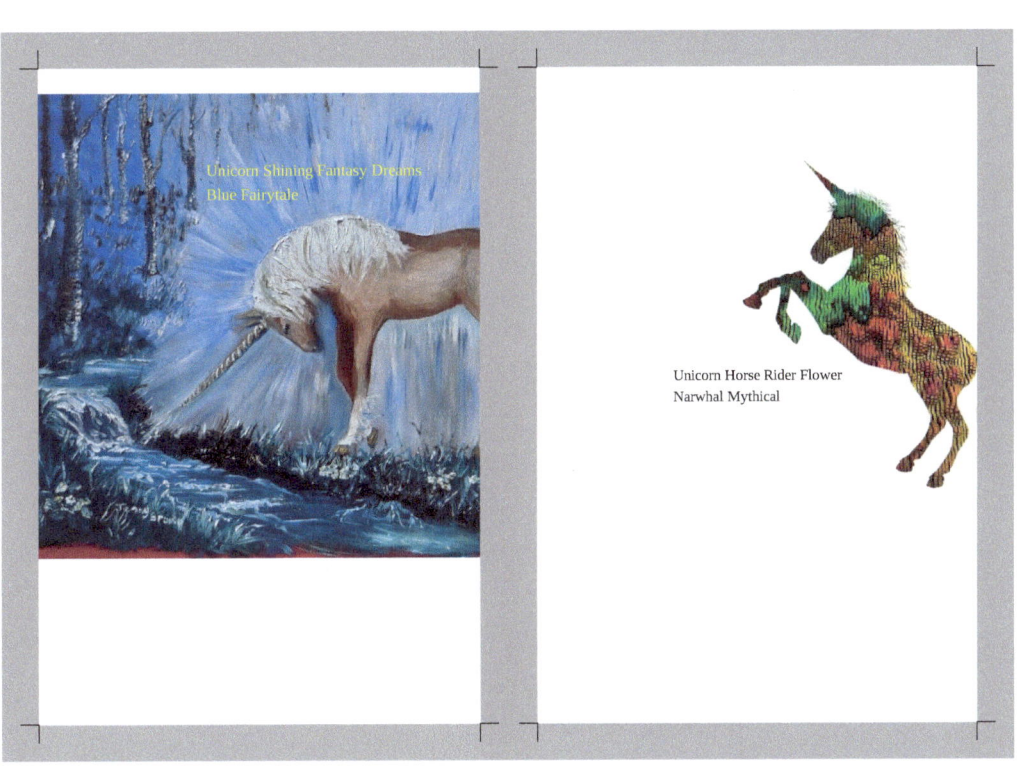

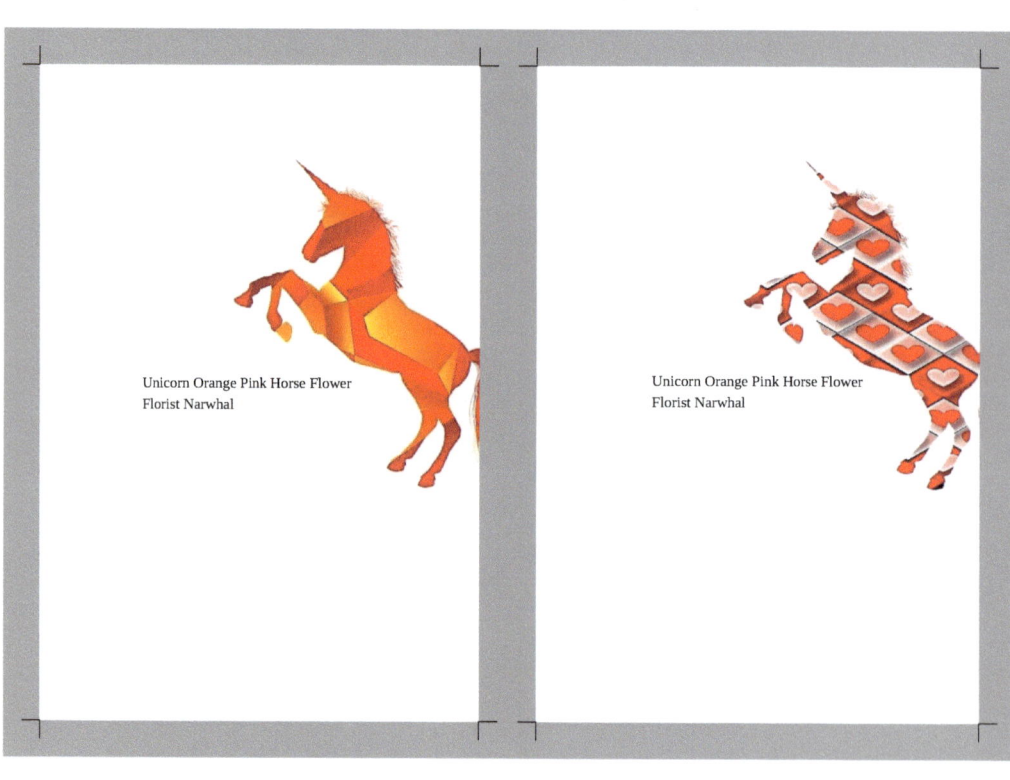

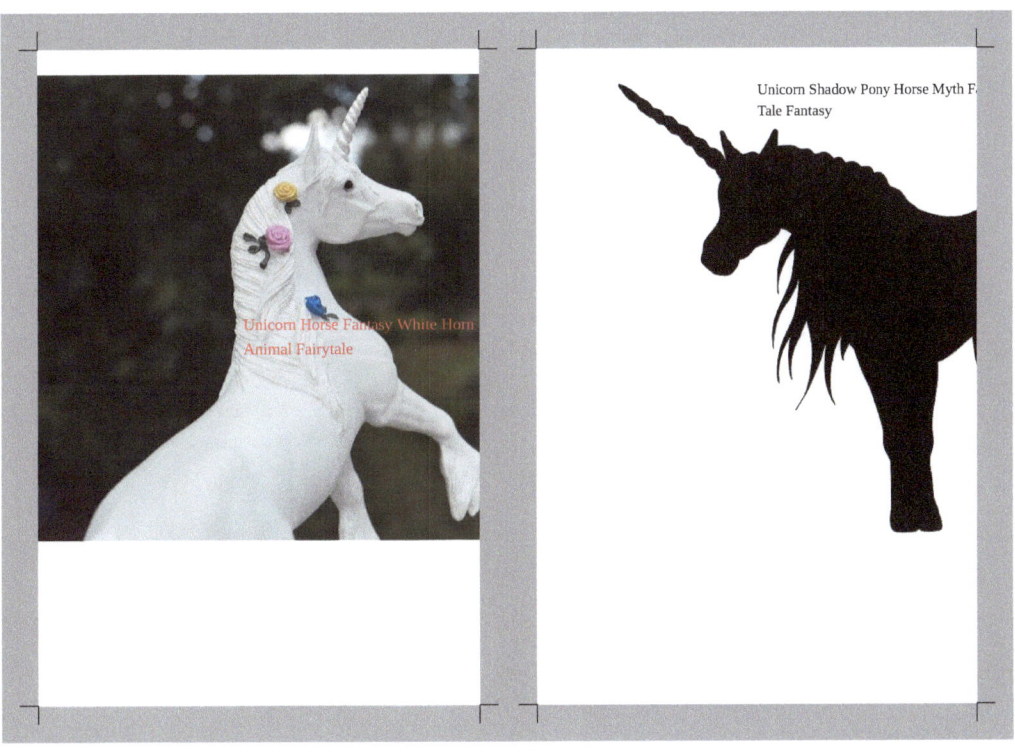

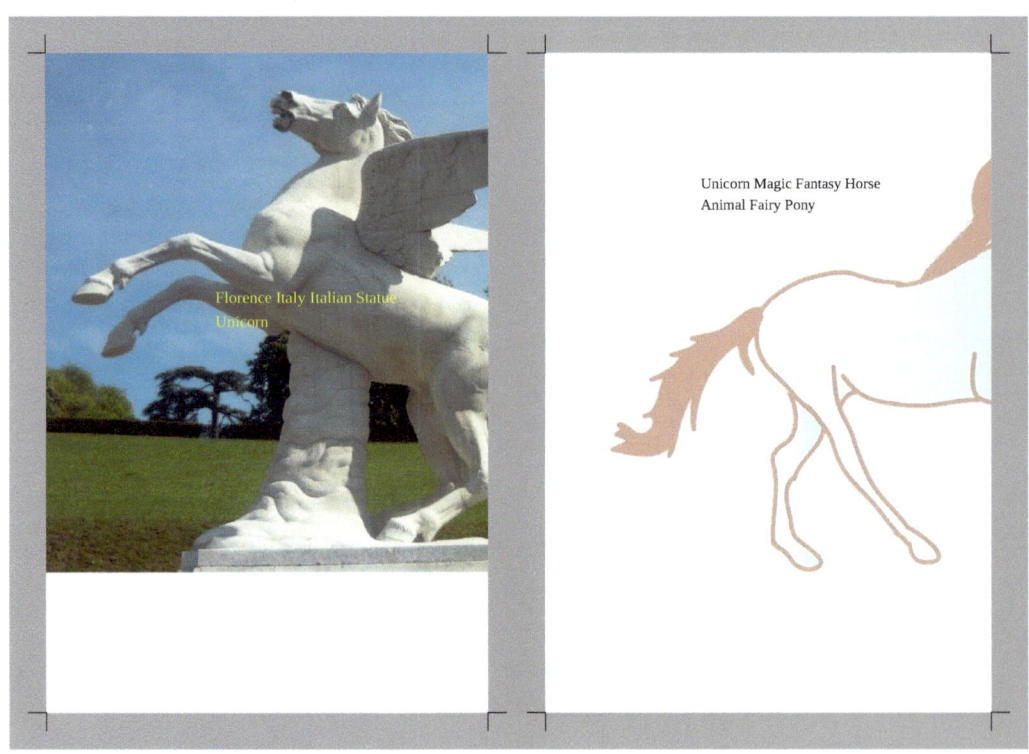

Florence Italy Italian Statue Unicorn

Unicorn Magic Fantasy Horse Animal Fairy Pony

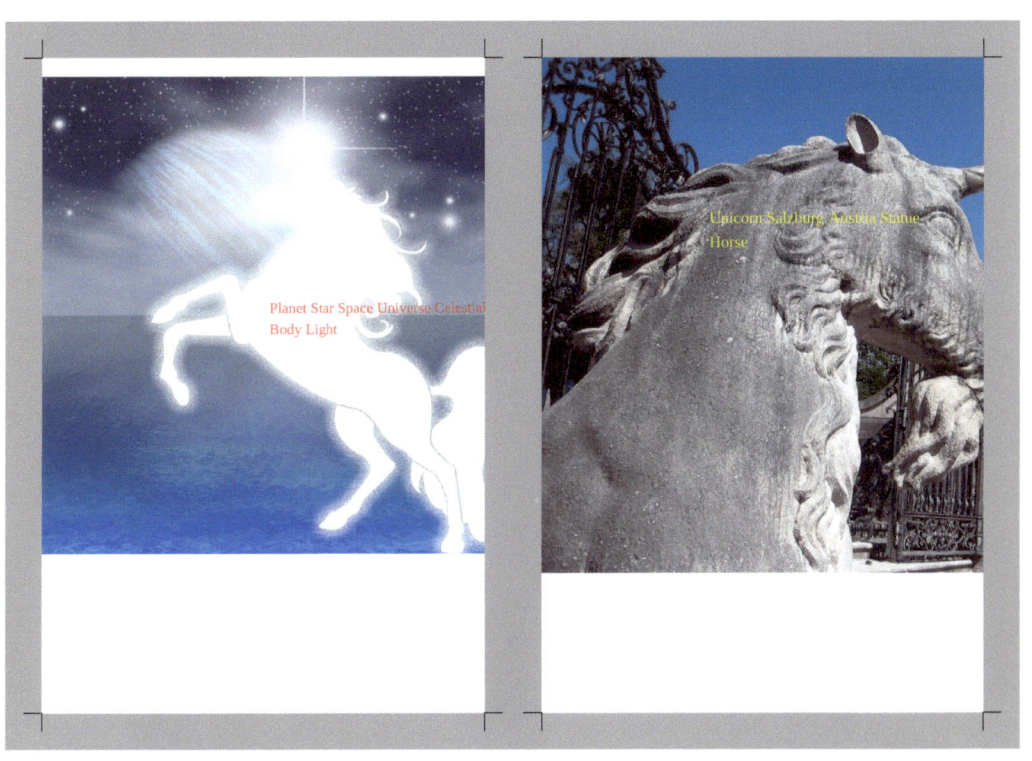

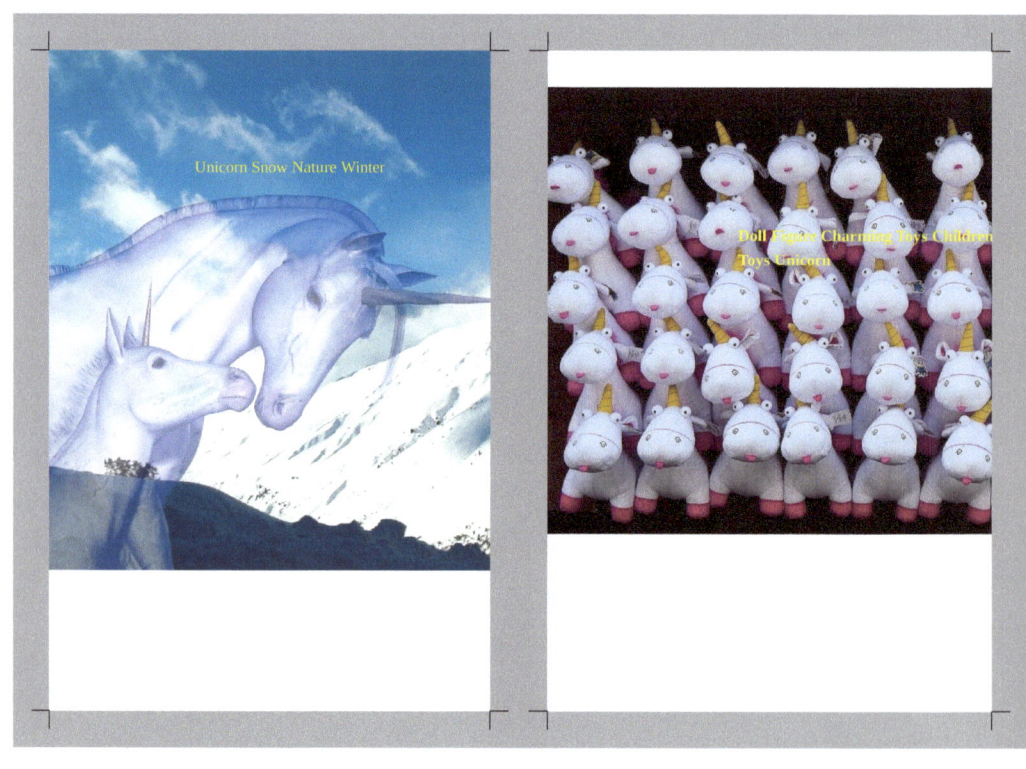

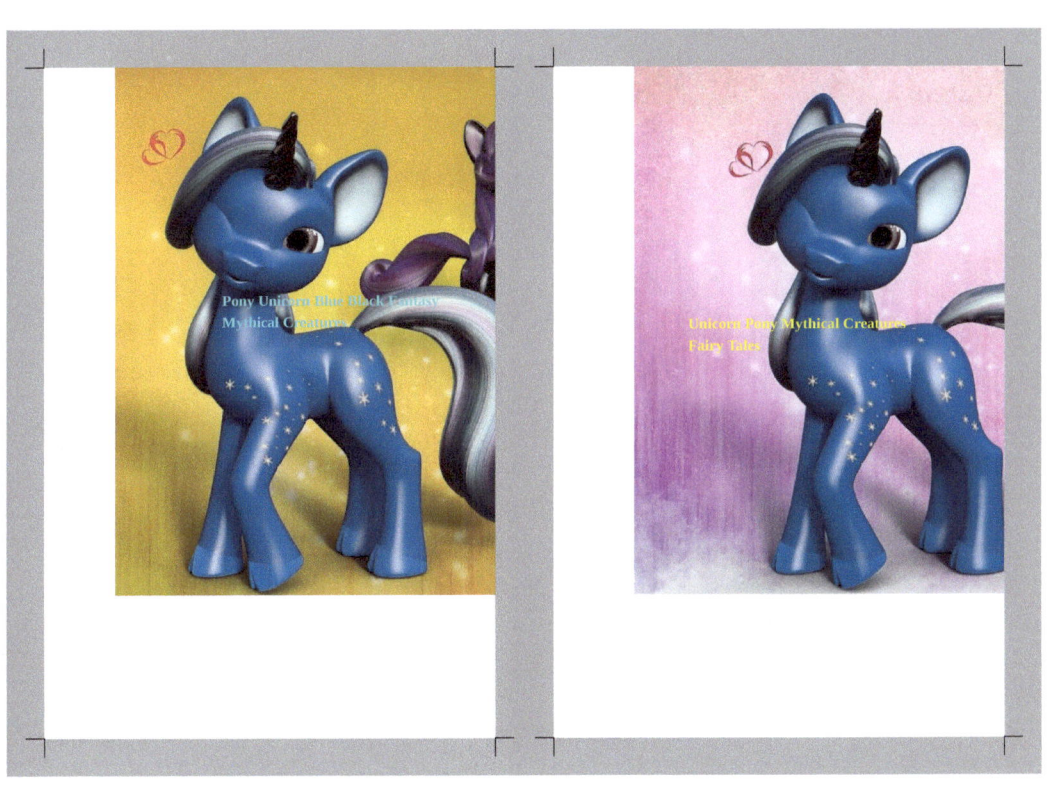

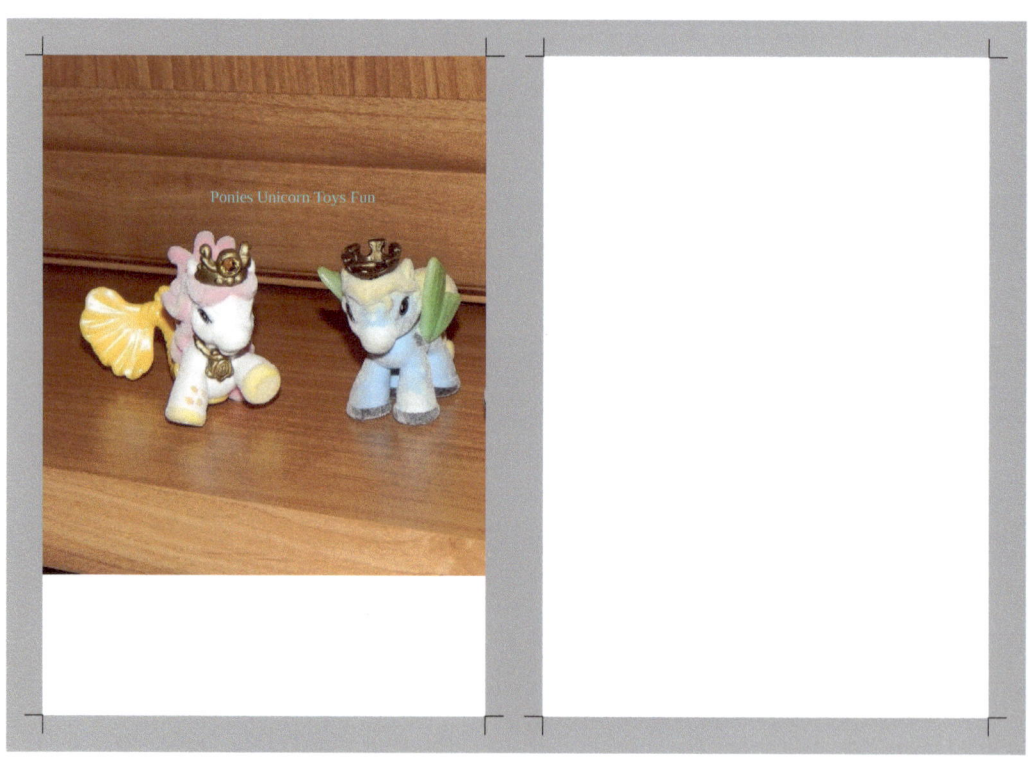

Ponies Unicorn Toys Fun

Proof

www.ingramcontent.com/pod-product-compliance
Lightning Source LLC
Chambersburg PA
CBHW040358220526
45473CB00021B/2563